How the U.S.
Got into Agriculture

How the U.S.
Got into Agriculture

And Why It Can't Get Out

David Rapp

Congressional Quarterly Inc.
1414 22nd Street N.W.
Washington, D.C. 20037

Congressional Quarterly Inc.

Congressional Quarterly Inc., an editorial research service and publishing company, serves clients in the fields of news, education, business, and government. It combines specific coverage of Congress, government, and politics by Congressional Quarterly with the more general subject range of an affiliated service, Editorial Research Reports.

Congressional Quarterly publishes the *Congressional Quarterly Weekly Report* and a variety of books, including college political science textbooks under the CQ Press imprint and public affairs paperbacks on developing issues and events. CQ also publishes information directories and reference books on the federal government, national elections, and politics, including the *Guide to Congress,* the *Guide to the U.S. Supreme Court,* the *Guide to U.S. Elections,* and *Politics in America.* The *CQ Almanac,* a compendium of legislation for one session of Congress, is published each year. *Congress and the Nation,* a record of government for a presidential term, is published every four years.

CQ publishes *The Congressional Monitor,* a daily report on current and future activities of congressional committees, and several newsletters including *Congressional Insight,* a weekly analysis of congressional action, and *Campaign Practices Reports,* a semimonthly update on campaign laws.

An electronic online information system, Washington Alert, provides immediate access to CQ's databases of legislative action, votes, schedules, profiles, and analyses.

Photo credits: cover - Jim Pickerell; pp. 2, 9, 12, 23, 36, 40, 55, 71, 77, 94, 103, 121, 140, 143, 159 - U.S. Department of Agriculture; p. 8 - National Portrait Gallery, Smithsonian Institution, Washington, D.C. (detail); pp. 42, 60, 85, 87, 105, 133 - Ken Heinen; pp. 43, 98, 150, 152 - Marty LaVor; p. 47 - Library of Congress; p. 48 - Paul Conklin; pp. 53, 73 - AP/Wide World Photos; pp. 65, 66, 111 - *Washington Post;* p. 68 - Sue Klemens; pp. 79, 151 - Teresa Zabala; p. 91 - Karen Ruckman; pp. 107, 170 - Art Stein; p. 166 - Black Star/Eiji Miyazawa.

Library of Congress Cataloging-in-Publication Data

Rapp, David, 1951-
    How the U.S. got into agriculture : and why it can't get out /
David Rapp.
        p.   cm.
    Bibliography: p.
    Includes index.
    ISBN 0-87187-457-1
    1. Agriculture and state--United States--History.   I. Title.
II. Title: How the US got into agriculture.
HD1761.R25 1988
338.1'873--dc19

88-18891
CIP

(handwritten call number:) Ref HD 1761 .R25 1988

For my mother and father

Table of Contents

Tables and Figures

Tables

Figures

Preface

In May and June of 1988, an unusually widespread heat spell settled over the United States. Much of the country went without rain for weeks on end as temperatures shot upward—and then stayed—in the 90s and 100s. The hot and dry conditions posed damaging consequences for the agricultural heartland, where fragile new crops had just been planted. Farmers from east coast to west, it was feared, would be helpless in the face of a seemingly unending drought. Farmland from Oregon to Iowa to Georgia was parched. Rivers and creekbeds were drying up. Even on the mighty Mississippi, the lifeline of the nation's agricultural transportation network, barge traffic halted as the water level dropped to record lows.

Into this bleak situation rushed the U.S. government. Before any crop had been destroyed—before a single farmer had reported a dollar's loss—Congress and the Reagan administration stood ready to come to the rescue. Election-minded lawmakers furiously began to prepare legislation to ensure their farmer-constituents against any potential crop failures. The administration responded just as quickly by promising to use all the disaster-relief authority it possessed. "We are not going to allow hundreds of thousands of the nation's best farmers and ranchers to be thrown out of business by a drought," Patrick J. Leahy, the chairman of the Senate Agriculture Committee, told his colleagues on the Senate floor. "We are going to make sure they stay in business."

The United States has long had the most efficient food and fiber production system in the world. And even in hard times, U.S. agriculture has thrived. It takes nothing away from hard-working American farmers to point out that this prosperity is largely a result of the helping hand of the federal government. Since the early 1900s, Congress and successive administrations have financed and nurtured the farm economy.

Yet after seventy-five years of intervention in agriculture, federal policy makers are still wrestling over just how much the government should be involved in the nation's farming enterprises. They are as perplexed by the "farm question" as they were at the turn of the century, when the federal role began in earnest. Moreover, the steep price tag that has recently been attached to farm programs—a record $26 billion for price supports alone in 1986—has forced many people to doubt the government's very ability to manage the agricultural economy. How did the government come to play such a large part in farming? Why do lawmakers feel such a strong commitment to agriculture and to farmers? What can be done to control farm spending?

Federal participation in agriculture is an established fact of political life. It has become entrenched by generations of lawmakers who have devoted large sums of taxpayer money to farm programs and received significant political payoffs in return. Indeed, in terms of pure political gamesmanship, the making of farm policy is one of the most intense and intrigue-filled activities of Congress. The often-partisan showdowns in the House and Senate over agriculture can be a thing to behold, but they are that way for a reason: Farm programs, unlike most federal subsidies, have a direct connection to their recipients. Federal farm payments are not filtered down to the beneficiaries through state and local governments, as are food stamps, welfare, education and highway grants, and other forms of federal largess. Farm payments go from the Agriculture Department to farmers themselves. Politicians on Capitol Hill and in the White House know that their day-to-day decisions on farm policy have direct—and immediate—impact on the lives and livelihoods of their farmer-constituents. And as a result, they know that the political stakes associated with farm policy questions can be huge. The farm vote can determine whether Democrats or Republicans will control the U.S. Senate, and it can seal the fate of a presidential candidate in a party's nominating process.

Yet when people unfamiliar with farm policy actually start digging into agriculture programs, something strange beings to happen. Mouths fall agape, nostrils flare, and eyes glaze over.

Images of Rube Goldbergian complexity spring to mind. Even tax economists, pension lawyers, and defense contractors—experts in their own right at maneuvering through arcane and jargon-filled federal statutes—stand back in awe and envy at the ingeniously crafted fine print of farm law.

This book is designed for lay readers interested in understanding the underlying politics and economics of farm policy. It is for those urban voters who see their pipeline to Washington being cut while farmers continue to reap huge benefits from the federal government, as well as for those rural citizens who want to know how their representatives work for them in Washington. It is for those citizens who wonder why many people in the world are starving at the same time U.S. farmers are producing twice as much food as this nation can consume. It is also for those students of politics who cannot understand how a dwindling number of farmer-voters maintain such tremendous political power.

In undertaking this project, I set out to describe the forces that shape agriculture policy and to show what some of the real, if not so apparent, issues are. The farm question is an age-old topic in national politics, but perhaps more importantly, it is now clear that the antagonists in the farm debate will be arguing their cases for a long time to come. I hope this book will illuminate the reasons.

The book begins with an overview of the government's efforts to come to the aid of farmers and of the pressures working on farm-state legislators to justify the expense of farm programs and to devise policies that actually help struggling farmers. Chapter 1 deals with the reverence Americans and lawmakers feel for the ideal of the "family farmer" and how that image has driven policy decisions over generations, but particularly over the past decade.

As outlined in Chapter 2, the simple reason farm spending has spiraled out of control is that more and more farmers began signing up for federal farm program benefits at a time when commodity prices and land values were plunging downward and export prospects remained bleak. In the meantime, the purpose of farm programs shifted from a policy of price stabilization to an effort to supply farmers with direct income subsidies.

Chapter 3 discusses the two opposing viewpoints that have existed in the policy debate over agriculture since the 1920s— one favoring government intervention, the other supporting a free-market approach. The question of whether farmers would be better served by receiving government help or by being forced to survive on their own has long divided agricultural policy makers. In all probability it will continue to do so.

The agriculture community is made up of competing geographical, political, and crop interests. As described in Chapter 4, traditional fixtures of the farm lobby—umbrella groups such as the American Farm Bureau Federation and the National Farmers Union still work on behalf of large numbers of farmers. But individual commodity organizations—representing wheat, corn, cotton, rice, and other growers—now also play a major role in shaping U.S. farm policy. Each organization will go its own way to meet the demands of its constituency, yet collectively they have found ways to come together, especially when the entire farm policy structure is under attack.

The Commodity Credit Corporation (CCC), a unique governmental entity used by the Agriculture Department to distribute price- and income-support payments to farmers, and Rep. Jamie L. Whitten, chairman of the House Appropriations Committee, are the subjects of Chapter 5. Whitten and other farm-state legislators have used the CCC and the peculiar way it operates to protect farm programs and, at the same time, hold sway over a wide variety of congressional spending decisions. In the process, the largely unknown Mississippian has become one of the most powerful legislators in Washington.

Chapter 6 shifts the focus from farm payment programs to the equally significant policy issue of farm debt. The system of public and private lending institutions set up by the government to make credit available to farmers in the hard times of the 1930s is having difficulty adapting to the farm economy of the 1980s. More than half of the $200 billion worth of debts held by U.S. farmers are government-related loans. Most of those are issued by the Farm Credit System, a nominally private institution. But, as a creature of Congress, the Farm Credit System has been operating on the assumption that the government will back up its bad debt. It was in danger of going bankrupt in 1987 and 1988 until an unusual alliance of rural and urban interests in Congress, recognizing the danger the system's collapse could pose to the nation's entire financial structure, came to the rescue with a $4 billion bailout plan. In the process, Congress advanced the government's role in agricultural credit farther than ever before.

An important element of farm law often overlooked in congressional debates is the broad discretionary powers Congress cedes to the executive branch in carrying out farm policy. In a prime example of that power, the Reagan administration in 1986 created a new farm payment scheme—the Agriculture Department's program of giving certificates, redeemable for government-owned grain, in lieu of cash to farmers. This payment-in-kind (PIK) program, examined in Chapter 7, quickly became the centerpiece of the nation's farm policy. The appeal of the "new currency" was unanticipated by the administration, which eventually issued PIK certificates worth $18 billion into the farm economy between 1986 and early 1988. While popular with farmers, who found new ways to make money with the certificates, the program also provided a means for the administration to strengthen its grip over the farm marketplace.

The United States is not the only country pumping billions of tax dollars into its agricultural economy. The twelve-nation European Economic Community, Australia, Canada, and Japan also subsidize their farmers, and they are experiencing the same budgetary and political pressures as the U.S. government. Chapter 8 reviews a fundamental conflict between U.S. foreign policy and its farm policy—support of a free-market world economy while subsidizing farm exports. A new round of international trade talks in Geneva, Switzerland, under the auspices of the General Agreement on Tariffs and Trade (GATT), has become the focal point of efforts by the Reagan administration and others to reduce government subsidies in agriculture. But competing interests will make an agreement as difficult to achieve in the international arena as in the U.S. Congress.

Many people have helped and encouraged me since I began this project, and I want to take the opportunity to thank them here. My colleagues on the *Congressional Quarterly Weekly Report* staff were a particular source of inspiration. They wanted to understand what was going on in agriculture and would constantly ask me to tell them what concerned citizens were "supposed" to think about farm policy. Their questions provided me with my first ideas for a primer on agriculture, which evolved into a series of stories that appeared in the *Weekly Report* in 1987. This book grew from that series.

People in Capitol Hill agriculture circles know that few people understand the intricacies of farm policy, and fortunately for reporters like me, they generally are willing to take the time to explain the many nuances. For their patience and accessibility I am grateful to the staffs of the House and Senate Agriculture committees, the Appropriations subcommittees on Agriculture, the agriculture experts of the Budget committees, the Congressional Research Service, and the Congressional Budget Office. Two persons in this group deserve my special thanks: Bernard Brenner, the retired press secretary of the House Agriculture Committee, was doubtlessly the most helpful and tireless press aide on Capitol Hill. He went out of his way to help all of us covering farm issues, and he came to my rescue more times than I should admit. Gene Moos, agriculture adviser to House majority leader Thomas S. Foley, was forever considerate and patient while providing cogent and reliable perspectives on the inner workings of farm legislation.

The men and women who work for the many agricultural trade associations in Washington also became valued sources of information and insight, and they were generally friendly and helpful in responding to my inquiries.

My appreciation also goes to a number of editors, past and present, on the *Weekly Report* staff. They are the unsung heroes of our organization. Bob Merry, Kathy Gest, Michael Glennon, Steve Gettinger, Mark Willen, Martha Angle, and Marsha Canfield provided guidance and direction to my stories. My special devotion goes to John Cranford, who nursed me through many a nervous deadline during the 1985 farm bill debates. I am also indebted to John, and to my friends Jasper Womack and Joe Kennedy, for reading the early manuscript and making many helpful suggestions. Thanks also to the editors and staff of the CQ Book Department for their many contributions to this project.

I also want to thank my friends in the "ag pack"—the many reporters who cover agriculture in Washington. They were exceptional to work with because of their relentless desire to understand the subject they were writing about. I learned much about farm policy just from listening to their conversations.

Finally, thanks to my wife, Lee Anne, for forgiving my dereliction of household chores on so many evenings and weekends, and for providing unquestioned encouragement and support for my work. I owe everything to her love.

How the U.S.
Got into Agriculture

Chapter 1

The Politics of Food

Nearly a decade after Ronald Reagan was elected president on a pledge to get the federal government "off the backs" of American taxpayers, one part of the economy still wholly dependent on their support is agriculture. U.S. farmers were relying more on federal subsidies at the close of the 1980s than when the Reagan administration came to power in January 1981. The cost of those subsidies had grown to staggering, multibillion dollar proportions, high enough to foment widespread public outrage and to put all of agriculture under attack. Yet even "Reaganomics," the economic semirevolution that brought about the largest federal spending and tax cuts in U.S. history, was powerless to reverse the trend. In fact, Reagan and a more-than-willing Congress pursued a course in agriculture that virtually ensured the United States would proceed into the 1990s with more, not less, government intervention in American farmers' lives and work.

This is the result of a uniquely political, as well as economic, paradox. A dwindling number of farm men and women continue each year to produce twice as much food and fiber as the rest of the nation can consume. Yet every attempt to cut their tether to the U.S. Treasury has been summarily rejected by Congress and, by extension, American voters. Agriculture producers continue to be fostered through good times and protected in bad ones, if for no other reason than that, in the White House, on Capitol Hill, and throughout the country, there is an abiding reverence for that fading hero of American life known as the "family farmer." Seemingly, this descendant of the American pioneer remains a precious national icon.

Americans and lawmakers retain a reverence for the "family farm," like this one in Loganville, Wis.

When a new president takes office in January 1989 and confronts a mammoth $3 trillion national debt and annual $150 billion budget deficits—both bloated in large measure by uncontrolled "entitlement" subsidies for agriculture—one betting certainty is that the U.S. government's financial commitment to farmers will remain as unshakable as ever. One thing else is certain: The taxpaying citizens who help consume the great agricultural bounty of America's family farms will foot the bill.

A truism in agricultural circles is that American consumers get the best food bargain in the world. Food prices are indeed lower in the United States than anywhere else, taking up only 11 percent of the average citizen's household expense budget in 1984. A family in West Germany, on the other hand, spends nearly 18 percent of its income on groceries. In Japan the food bill approaches 20 percent—almost twice as much as in the United States—and in the Soviet Union it is nearly 26 percent. In many developing countries, the ratio is even higher, reaching a peak of 60 percent in the small West African nation of Niger. (See Table 1-1.)

Many countries support their farmers with policies that artificially force up farm—and thus food—prices; that is, they subsidize agriculture at the expense of consumers. The United States, meanwhile, maintains a variety of farm programs that generally has kept food prices down. Though many other forces are at play, including international economic events well outside

Table 1-1 Comparative International Food Expenditures

Country	Percentage of personal consumption expenditures for food	Country	Percentage of personal consumption expenditures for food
United States	11.0	Cyprus	28.6
Zimbabwe	12.7	Malta	29.0
Canada	13.4	Spain	29.2
United Kingdom	14.5	Colombia	31.2
Netherlands	15.0	Yugoslavia	31.2
Australia	15.5	Mexico	31.7
Luxembourg	16.1	Portugal	33.1
Denmark	17.2	Malaysia	33.8
West Germany	17.6	Ecuador	34.5
France	17.9	El Salvador	35.2
Austria	18.5	Bolivia	35.5
Hong Kong	18.8	Sudan	35.8
Sweden	18.8	Korea	36.1
Belgium	19.1	Jamaica	36.8
Japan	19.9	Poland	36.8
Norway	20.0	Greece	36.9
Finland	20.1	Jordan	38.0
Switzerland	20.2	Thailand	38.7
Bahamas	22.3	Venezuela	39.6
Puerto Rico	22.6	Honduras	41.4
Singapore	22.6	Kenya	41.4
Israel	23.1	Sri Lanka	49.2
Ireland	23.8	Philippines	51.7
Italy	25.6	China	52.6
USSR	25.6	Sierra Leone	53.0
Fiji	25.8	India	53.1
South Africa	26.4	Ghana	53.6
Hungary	27.9	Niger	61.6

Source: U.S. Department of Agriculture, Economic Research Service, *National Food Review,* Fall 1987.

Note: Figures are as of 1984 except for Zimbabwe, Fiji, Colombia, Yugoslavia, Jordan, and Honduras, 1983; Ireland, Malta, Spain, Jamaica, and Poland, 1982; Bahamas, 1981; Portugal, Sudan, Kenya, Sierra Leone, and Niger, 1980; Bolivia, 1979; and El Salvador, Ghana, and Malaysia, 1978.

the sway of the U.S. or any single government, the low food bill in the United States is an important result of the way federal farm subsidies work—or do not work, as the case may be.

But then, American consumers pay a different price for this "cheap food policy," as farmers like to call it. The cost of farm price-support programs alone went from an average of $3 billion a year in the 1970s, to a record $26 billion in 1986. Another $5 billion to $7 billion a year went into other agricultural credit and support services financed by the Department of Agriculture. In fiscal 1986 the total amounted to more than 15 percent of the unprecedented $221 billion budget deficit incurred by the federal government. A year later, these farm programs cost another $27 billion, and even as Congress and the White House struggled to pare down the deficit in those and succeeding years, farm subsidies were expected to cost an average of $20 billion a year at least through 1991. In other words, U.S. citizens will be paying through taxes for any advantage the consumer manages to get on grocery bills. (See Table 1-2.)

This is the historic bargain of American food and agriculture policy. It has brought together consumers, who want low food prices, and farmers, who want control over their markets and an assurance of stable commodity prices. Seventy-five years after the first federally subsidized loans were made so farmers could buy their own farmland, and fifty years after the first federally financed price-support program was created as a "temporary" remedy for the unstable, depression-rocked agricultural economy, American farmers remain the most efficient producers of food in the world. No other country has been able to match the United States' rapid growth in agricultural technology and production capacity. No other country has been able to provide its populace with such "security" in food production, at so little cost to the end-users themselves. In the meantime, however, American farmers have gotten used to Uncle Sam's doting methods of protection. You might say they expect nothing less.

Political Power

Although the 4.9 million working farmers in the United States now make up only 2 percent of the population, they continue to hold such power and influence in Congress and in the White House that neither the Democratic nor the Republican party, for the most part, has dared challenge the basic

Table 1-2 Net Outlays for Price Supports and Related Activities, 1934-1987

Fiscal year	Net expenditure[a] (in millions)	Fiscal year	Net expenditure[a] (in millions)
1934	$ 162	1962	$ 2,052
1935	−60	1963	3,117
1936	33	1964	3,175
1937	−112	1965	2,648
1938	−185	1966	1,536
1939	136	1967	1,690
1940	211	1968	3,203
1941	347	1969	4,121
1942	242	1970	3,777
1943	−193	1971	2,822
1944	225	1972	3,983
1945	471	1973	3,555
1946[b]	1,044	1974	1,004
1947	432	1975	575
1948	−204	1976	1,014
1949	56	19TQ[c]	452
1950	1,606	1977	3,809
1951	−782	1978	5,656
1952	−241	1979	3,612
1953	1,831	1980	2,752
1954	1,333	1981	4,036
1955	3,097	1982	11,652
1956	2,939	1983	18,851
1957	1,144	1984	7,316
1958	1,054	1985	17,683
1959	2,850	1986	25,841
1960	1,561	1987	22,408
1961	1,331		

Source: U.S. Department of Agriculture.

Note: Figures include commodity loans and purchases, direct payments, interest, direct export credit, storage facility loans, storage and handling, and operating expenses.

[a] Minus sign (−) denotes net receipt.
[b] Fifteen months.
[c] Transition quarter.

premise that the government has a responsibility to support family farm enterprises. At stake are the hearts, minds, and votes of a pivotal special interest group spread throughout the nation's breadbasket.

Farmers occupy important political and financial positions

in nearly every state and in a large percentage of congressional districts, where they are usually well-organized and well-versed in making their feelings and opinions known to political office seekers. Agricultural interests also spread far beyond the farm, embracing a host of farm equipment, seed, and fertilizer suppliers, truckers, traders, rural bankers, and local shopkeepers, who together with farmers make up slightly more than one-fifth of the nation's labor force and produce goods and services totaling nearly one-fifth of the U.S. gross national product. While the individual interests within the nation's huge food and fiber system often clash, this economic universe begins with, and always revolves around, the farmer. (See Figure 1-1.)

The political importance of this fact cannot be overstated. Republicans and Democrats alike recognize that the balance of power in Congress and in the White House often hangs on how their parties fair in the agricultural heartland. When he was campaigning for president, Ronald Reagan made bold declarations about creating a "free-market" economy for agriculture, proposing to wean farmers completely from their dependence on federal largess before the end of the century. It was a message that played well at the time with irate taxpayers as well as disgruntled farmers, many of whom were doing very well financially without the help of the government (and were bitter about President Jimmy Carter's imposition of a grain embargo against the Soviet Union). But Reagan's assertions appeared contradictory—if not hypocritical—in view of his administration's steady softening of its early, hardline positions on cutting back farm subsidies and its evident willingness over the course of Reagan's two terms in office to pursue blatantly interventionist policies in agriculture. If Reagan's goal was to shore up the farm economy, the real object, by virtue of his actions, was to help farm-state Republican candidates on election day.

Urban Democrats, meanwhile, have been equally shameless in excoriating the high cost of farm subsidies, as if their own partisan voting habits in Congress had nothing to do with perpetuating and even expanding them. The party made farm issues an early rallying point for the 1986 congressional elections, when Democrats regained control of the Senate with the help of upset victories in several key Midwestern and Southern farm states. Similar appeals to rural sentiments were voiced in 1988 by Democratic presidential candidates, who hoped to capitalize on Reagan's increasingly negative ratings in farm country.

Figure 1-1 Farming-Oriented Congressional Districts

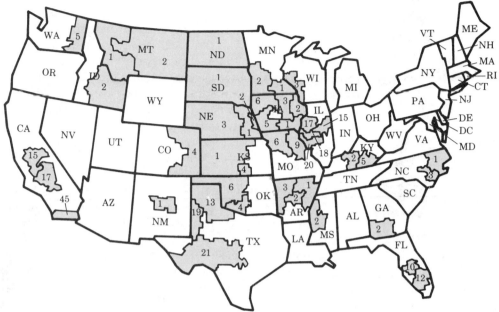

Source: Adapted from Bernal Green and Thomas Carlin, "Where Farming Really Counts: A Surprising Tally of Communities Where Farms Still Dominate," *Choices* (premiere issue, 1986), 31.

Note: A district with its number entered indicates that a third or more of its counties are farming dependent. A farming dependent county depended on farming for a fifth or more of its earned income, 1975-1979.

A Long History

Farmers have long held hypnotic sway over politicians. The populist movements of the 1860s, 1880s, and 1890s were founded upon agrarian discontent, and it was the growing awareness of farmers' economic power that eventually transformed an American political landscape dominated by eastern financial interests to one where rural and western concerns had to be accommodated. As the country expanded westward, the federal government in Washington, D.C., began to focus directly on farm interests. Congress created a special banking system for agriculture in 1916, and then, during the Great Depression of the 1930s, President Franklin D. Roosevelt hinged many of his New Deal initiatives on new credit-subsidy and price-support programs for farmers and ranchers.

7

President Franklin D. Roosevelt's New Deal programs made agriculture a key beneficiary in the government's effort to bring the economy out of the depression-rocked 1930s.

During the depression there were nearly seven million farms in the United States, and farm families still made up nearly a third the nation's population. What is more, hard times in agriculture were leading struggling farmers to commit desperate acts, forcing even skeptical policy makers to take their claims seriously. One mob threatened to hang a federal judge in protest against farm foreclosures. Other groups overturned milk trucks, picketed packing plants, and boycotted farm sales. "The mood was ominous," wrote Don Paarlberg, an agricultural economist at Purdue University who was a farmer during the New Deal era. "There was anger, frustration, and insistence on action. The Great Depression was worldwide. In Italy and Germany representative government was replaced by dictatorships. The American political and economic systems were threatened."

The condition of U.S. agriculture has changed dramatically since then. Over much of the twentieth century farmers have been one of the most productive and innovative sectors of the U.S. economy. The past fifty years have seen agriculture grow faster than other industries and, until the 1970s at least, faster than agricultural productivity in other countries. Yet despite massive taxpayer infusions into the farm economy (some say, as a result of them), the U.S. agricultural sector was experiencing in the 1980s its most severe crisis since the depression. The instability of commodity prices and trading relationships, the ever-troubled financial condition of many farm families and rural banks, and the continuing inability of federal farm programs to produce any lasting solutions have made U.S. policy seem chaotic and inept. As a result, agriculture has attracted more than just esoteric interest in this country, and it has taken on an ever-increasing importance to all countries of the world.

Yet the questions that began cropping up in the 1980s about federal agricultural policy suggest that budget makers in Congress and the White House were caught unawares by the meteoric cost of farm programs, not to mention the problems associated with their expense. The $26 billion price-tag for basic price-support programs in fiscal 1986 did wake up more than a few switch-sleepers, however. Also sparking new attention on farm policy were reports that a number of already well-to-do farmers were receiving million-dollar payments from the government, while small- and mid-sized farms were falling into bankruptcy and going out of business at rates unheard of since the 1930s.

But in truth, few lawmakers representing areas outside the farm community seemed to know or understand the causes of the farm budget crisis. Mostly they had not paid much heed to farm issues, so long as agriculture programs maintained the old bargain between consumer and farm interests and kept down the cost of food at the grocery store. They also did not really care about farm issues, so long as the rural factions of each party kept farm policy in some semblence of order, then delivered the farm vote on election day at relatively little cost to the taxpayer. These rural factions were remarkably successful for decades, until the part about cost-to-taxpayers got incredibly out of hand.

Around 1985, however, urban lawmakers and their consumer-oriented constituents began to take special notice of the

Farmland prices collapsed in the midst of the Great Depression, forcing the government to come to the rescue with new credit and price-support programs.

9

farm spending crisis, particularly as it applied to the ballooning federal deficit. As the Reagan administration successfully chopped away at other domestic programs created under the Democrats' New Deal and Great Society campaigns, the billions of dollars still going into farm programs took on even larger proportions. The shrinking federal pie prompted nonrural members of Congress and big-city voters to question the government's basic role in agriculture. In newspaper editorials, election campaigns, and congressional debates, agriculture was put under a harsh new spotlight. The public in general turned a quizzical and highly skeptical eye on the old consumer-farmer compact.

Search for Answers

Two questions inflame the new debate: Why did spending for farm programs jump six-fold in the five years between 1981 and 1986? And, how could it be cut back to size?

A third question, a logical outgrowth of the first two, has been nearly as pervasive and just as perplexing: Will the expensive marriage between farmer and government, now going on seventy-five years, ever end?

At the heart of all these questions is one basic issue: the federal government's commitment to agriculture and to farmers. Here is why neither Congress nor the White House is likely to abandon that commitment in the years to come:

● The cost of farm programs skyrocketed because more and more farmers—even those who once spurned federal help— began signing up for farm programs in the 1980s. Now firmly on board, they are not likely to jump back into the uncertain waters of the free market anytime soon.

● Since the early 1970s the agricultural economy has been buffeted by national and international events totally outside of farmers' control. The government, for both economic and political reasons, was practically obliged to come to the rescue.

● Over the years a tenacious and tightly knit group of farm lobbyists and political operatives has learned to minimize the differences and capitalize on the mutual interests of its members, particularly when it comes to getting farm legislation through Congress.

● Farm-state legislators also have developed a power base in Congress that outweighs their numerical order in Congress and far exceeds their constituents' population in the nation. They have fifty years of arcane farm law working for them.

• Because farmers rely heavily on borrowed funds, they are in constant search of new capital. The government has become their principal creditor and landlord.

• The White House and the Agriculture Department, possessing virtually unbridled authority over the administration of farm programs, have established hands-on control over the agriculture economy in ways that make it practically impossible for them to let go.

• Since farm subsidies are a worldwide phenomenon, it has become clear that the only way the U.S. government can withdraw from the farm economy without putting American farmers at serious risk is if governments in other nations do likewise. What is equally clear, however, is that few ever will.

Farm Politics

The U.S. government has been deeply involved in agriculture since the beginning of the twentieth century. It has remained at least an equal partner in American farm enterprises by virtue of agriculture's once-dominant position in the nation's economy and, not coincidentally, a generally accepted view that a thriving food and fiber production system was a requisite building block for any aspiring world power. As the economy grew more complex after World War II, it also became an increasingly accepted view that the government had a responsibility to intervene and actively assist whatever segments of the country were unable to benefit fully from the new national wealth. American farm policy is largely a product of these social and economic attitudes.

For most of the century, farm programs in the United States followed a relatively consistent policy that was founded on two basic objectives: easier access to credit and higher commodity prices. Congress provided the means for the first when it created a Federal Land Bank system in 1916 devoted exclusively to lending money to farmers.

Then in 1933, as farm prices collapsed in the midst of the Great Depression, Congress and the White House entered the commodity market directly. Out of the New Deal came a system of price supports and production controls for farmers of major crops. They were designed to release only a specified amount

11

onto the domestic market at any one time and thus, it was hoped, yield more stable and higher prices for farmers.

From the beginning the government focused on basic field crops—wheat, feed grains, cotton, rice, sugar, peanuts, and tobacco—because they were the most prevalent farm products and the easiest to store for extended periods of time. A dairy program was added in 1948 to maintain a minimum price for milk "equivalents" (cheese, butter, and dry milk). No direct market intervention programs have been established for beef, pork, and poultry, or for minor field crops, fruits, and vegetables, although the government over the years has provided farmers of these commodities an array of tariff and marketing protections, as well as highly beneficial tax incentives.

Income Supports

During World War II and afterwards, the government alternately succeeded and failed at keeping prices stable, and by the 1960s a third concept of government involvement in agriculture began to dominate the picture: income support. Congress would make direct payments to farmers to make up the difference between low market prices and some "target price" deemed

The federal government has focused its price-support programs on storable commodities—wheat, feed grains, cotton, rice, sugar, tobacco, and even peanuts, pictured here.

more desirable.

Since the 1960s, the overriding question in congressional debates on farm policy was not whether the government should get involved in production control and supply management— that, as agricultural historian Willard W. Cochrane has written, "was a foregone conclusion." The leading issue was how much the government was willing to support farm incomes by making direct payments to farmers.

From the 1920s through 1960, government payments to farmers were a relatively negligible part of their overall earnings. Payments rarely reached as high as 10 percent of the average farm household's net cash income. Beginning in the 1960s, however, the government's share of farmers' incomes began to rise substantially. It averaged about 20 percent between 1965 and 1973 before falling back in the late 1970s and early 1980s. (See Table 1-3.)

In the mid-1980s, however, the government became a major contributor to farmers' incomes, to the extent that by 1987, when net farm income reached a high of $57 billion in the United States, $17 billion or 30 percent of the total was in the form of direct government payments.

These record payments have put politicians into an unusual bind. More than ever before, they are faced with the dilemma of whether to continue the government's active role in agriculture, at the price of even greater costs to the taxpayer, or to turn agriculture over to the free market, possibly at the risk of driving up food prices for consumers. Or—failing increases in either budget or prices—they would have to tolerate lower total farm income. The logic of the agriculture economy insists that if farm program costs must be reduced, then farm income must fall as a direct consequence, unless the costs of these programs can be transferred to the consumer through higher food prices. "This is the economic dilemma," wrote economist James T. Bonnen in 1965. "It is also a political dilemma since each of these variables—budget, consumer costs and farm income— involves politically potent interests."

Budgetary Impact

Still, the full ramifications of the government's income-support policy for farmers took awhile to set in. Market prices skyrocketed above government target prices in the late 1970s as

Table 1-3 Number of Farms and Income per Farm

Year or years	Number of farms (in thousands)	Net income per farm	Government payment per farm	Government payment as percentage of farm income
1910-1914 [a]	6,429	$ 598	$ 0	0
1925-1929 [a]	6,475	936	0	0
1935-1939 [a]	6,631	706	72	10
1945	5,967	1,894	124	7
1946	5,926	2,211	130	6
1947	5,871	2,606	53	2
1948	5,803	2,516	44	2
1949	5,722	2,289	33	1
1950	5,648	2,249	50	2
1951	5,428	2,727	53	2
1952	5,198	2,732	53	2
1953	4,983	2,830	43	2
1954	4,798	2,668	54	2
1955	4,654	2,621	49	2
1956	4,514	2,858	123	4
1957	4,372	2,722	232	9
1958	4,233	3,260	257	8
1959	4,097	3,051	166	5
1960	3,963	3,230	177	5
1961	3,825	3,582	390	11
1962	3,692	3,711	473	13
1963	3,572	3,807	475	12
1964	3,457	4,050	630	16
1965	3,356	4,380	734	17
1966	3,257	5,250	1,006	19
1967	3,162	4,775	973	20
1968	3,071	5,177	1,128	22
1969	3,000	6,033	1,264	21
1970	2,949	6,239	1,260	20
1971	2,902	6,203	1,084	17
1972	2,860	8,112	1,385	17
1973	2,823	12,752	923	7
1974	2,795	12,451	190	2
1975	2,521	11,741	320	3
1976	2,497	11,974	294	2
1977	2,456	11,360	740	7
1978	2,436	13,588	1,244	9
1979	2,432	13,734	566	4
1980	2,433	14,057	528	4
1981	2,434	13,476	794	6
1982	2,401	15,868	1,454	9
1983	2,370	15,654	3,922	25
1984	2,328	16,667	3,622	22
1985	2,275	20,791	3,387	16
1986	2,212	23,508	5,341	23
1987	2,200	25,909	7,727	30
1988	2,200	23,864	6,364	27

Sources: U.S. Department of Agriculture, Economic Research Service, *Economic Indicators of the Farm Sector: National Financial Summary, 1986;* and *Agricultural Outlook,* April 1988.

Note: A farm, as defined by the Bureau of the Census in 1978, is any place that has or would have had $1,000 or more in gross sales of farm products.

[a] Figures are averages for the five-year period.

a result of an export boom in agriculture, so farm price- and income-support programs were made generally inoperative. But the bottom soon dropped out of the export market and the farmland price began to plunge. By the early 1980s the price- and income-support policies established a decade earlier finally kicked in at full force.

Agriculture suddenly became the fastest-growing item in the federal budget during the years that President Reagan, along with a not-altogether reluctant Congress, was slashing away at nearly every other domestic spending program. By 1986 farm programs were the third largest benefit program in the government's domestic arsenal, next to Social Security and Medicare. And as time passed after the enactment of the 1985 farm bill, which was Congress's and the Reagan administration's most recent effort to get a handle on the unpredictable cost of farm programs, it became clear that spending on agriculture would not decline substantially for many years to come. Government—and taxpayer—support of farmers became the commitment of yet another generation.

Not surprisingly, then, farm spending took on new prominence in the intense debate in Congress over the federal budget deficit. Nonrural members who virtually ignored agriculture in the past began to focus on the farm budget crisis. "In my part of the country, if an industry can't cut the mustard, they close down," said one urban representative, Democrat Frank J. Guarini of New Jersey. His comment reflected a growing bitterness among Rust Belt members about the favored status and power that Farm Belt districts enjoyed in Washington. "Do we have too many farmers?" Guarini asked rhetorically at one House Budget Committee meeting. "Do we have $25 billion a year thrown at a problem that really has no solution?"

New Focus on Agriculture

Such questions about farm spending, which began popping up with more frequency in 1986 and 1987, have not gone away and are likely to intensify as Congress reassesses farm policy in 1989 and 1990. At bottom the questions reveal longstanding doubts about the government's role in agriculture. But they also show that a new political imperative has cracked the sanctified inner workings of the farm programs—money.

When a segment of government can get its hands on $20-

plus billion a year, it will attract a flock of special interest lobbies with different ideas on how to spend it. New faces will begin showing up at House and Senate Agriculture Committee meetings to find out what is going on and how to get in on the action. Consumer groups, conservationists, chemical manufacturers, bankers, and financial investors will try to stake their own claims to the agricultural dollar. Journalists, editorial writers, and students of politics will become more curious about the strange, symbiotic relationship between farmer and government.

For many who do not deal closely with farm programs (and for some who do), the cost and conduct of U.S. farm policy can be difficult to comprehend. Even Pete V. Domenici of New Mexico, the former chairman of and senior Republican on the Senate Budget Committee (and one of the most knowledgable experts on budget issues in Congress), was as perplexed as anyone when it came to agriculture policy. "Unfortunately, I don't see a consensus about how to change farm laws," he worried aloud early in 1986, when farm program spending hit its peak. "Lack of spending by the government is not the problem. More spending is certainly not the solution."

Suddenly, the old argument over how best to structure U.S. agriculture policy was being supplanted by an equally contentious debate about how much it costs to make one work. The change in emphasis threatened to shake up the urban-rural political alliances that have built up over decades and have managed to construct a useful, if tenuous, balance between competing farmer and consumer interests. "We've got to take a much closer look at what the nation gets for the farm dollar," said Florida Democrat Lawton Chiles when he took over as chairman of the Senate Budget Committee in early 1987. "If we want to get rid of the deficit, agriculture will have to take some cuts just like the rest of our programs."

The old alliance had been useful for two reasons. It put a safety net under farmers' incomes while ensuring that consumers had relatively low food prices. During the 1960s and 1970s, when farm program spending averaged less than $5 billion a year, farm income grew steadily, and supermarket prices remained low. American consumers got the twin benefits of cheap food and minimal tax burdens.

More significantly, perhaps, the urban-rural alliance created an equation for political opportunity for Democrats and

Republicans. They both have been successful at bringing farm and consumer interests together for their particular legislative and political objectives. There was good reason why the food stamp program, a cornerstone of the Great Society welfare programs of the 1960s, early on was made a part of the Department of Agriculture's annual budget, giving urban members a large interest in the success of appropriations for farm programs.

But the exploding cost of farm programs has altered the economic equation, and possibly the political one as well. The general rule of agriculture throughout the world is that farmers, to bolster their incomes, must get support from one of two sources: the marketplace or the government. If one does not take on most of the burden, the other one must. The underlying assumption, of course, is that farm income must be supported.

The potential for conflict between farmer, consumer, and budgetary interests has always existed, though it has only lately come into view. A tremor of the impending confrontation went through Congress in 1986 and 1987 when urban members pushed through legislation to place strict limits on the amount of farm program payments that any one farmer could receive. In 1986 they won approval for a bill to place a $250,000 per farm cap on government benefits, and when it became apparent that some farmers were merely dividing their farms into different corporate entities to get around the new payment restrictions, urban lawmakers came back the next year with legislation to tighten up the eligibility rules.

Another sign of the new political environment for farm programs was displayed by farm-state lawmakers themselves. Midwestern populists who were pushing for strict mandatory controls on farm production adopted a strategy that emphasized the lower cost of their program compared with the expensive, "market-oriented" policy that Congress adopted in 1985. They began pitching mandatory controls on their ability to reduce supply, raise farm prices, and subsequently cut budget costs. The trade-off would be that increasing farm prices leads to higher grocery prices. "We should reduce the exposure to the taxpayer, and the way you do that is to increase the exposure to the consumer," argued Sen. Edward Zorinsky of Nebraska before his death in 1987. "God forbid," he added sarcastically, "that the consumer should have to pay 1 percent more of his disposable income for food."

17

Seeds for Change

For a brief time in the mid-1980s, it seemed Congress might be ready to reexamine its views toward agriculture. Existing farm programs were due to expire at the end of 1985, and many officials in the Reagan administration saw an opportunity to begin a wholesale assault on the way the government propped up farm production. The administration had made such efforts before, with only occasional and incremental successes. But increasingly, price-support devices were being viewed on Capitol Hill, as well as among farm exporters, as more of a hindrance than a help to competing in foreign markets. Critics believed U.S. farm policy was keeping prices artificially above world market levels and forcing the government to buy up and store much of the stocks.

The administration wanted to lower price supports for major commodities to bring them in line with prevailing world prices and, it was hoped, make U.S. farmers more competitive in foreign markets and allow the government to rid itself of huge grain surpluses. Democratic leaders were willing to restructure price supports to keep them more attuned to market fluctuations, but they insisted on only modest reductions instead of completely breaking with existing policy promoted by the Reagan administration. "It's not a totally happy choice, but we have to make a move to more market-oriented [price-support] rates," said Thomas S. Foley, a Democrat from Washington who was the leading voice for agriculture in the House. "But at least we don't want anything as Draconian as the administration would have it."

But what looked in 1984 liked a receptive climate for major changes in agriculture policy quickly gave way in early 1985. The Catch-22 for farm-state legislators became obvious. Removing the price-support net from major commodities would force prices downward and cut farmers' incomes. As a result, efforts to rewrite farm policy became enmeshed in the competing interests and often conflicting goals of trying to craft a farm policy that would at once lower farm prices, bolster farmers' incomes, and cut government expenses. Stuffing all three into one package proved impossible.

Even though farm-state legislators were willing to consider changes in the way the government supported prices, they remained fiercely protective of other subsidy mechanisms that ensured farmers against losses accruing from the declining prices of their goods. They insisted on either starting new government programs for exports—subsidizing them as well as creating more markets for them—or maintaining a generous program of cash subsidies to guarantee stable incomes for farmers.

Whereas the White House began by talking about gradually doing away with subsidies, members of Congress ended up by discussing how to expand them. "We have lost our taste for great reforms," Dan Glickman, a Kansas Democrat on the House Agriculture Committee, said in June 1985 shortly after the process of crafting a new farm bill started. "The problem we face is we can't coalesce on any one option. It looks like we will end up with something more like the current programs than what the Reagan administration is talking about."

In a year when lowering budget deficits was the watchword in both the House and Senate, the two approaches for dealing with the farm crisis—income protection and export subsidies—appeared to be in direct conflict with the idea of cutting costs. Instead, the Agriculture committees were forced to choose between spending more money on export programs or spending more money on domestic income supports. They eventually chose something of both, though most of the emphasis remained on income supports.

Political Expediencies

President Reagan, ever conscious of his political base in the Midwestern breadbasket, had waited until after the November 1984 elections to offer his own austere blueprint for long-term farm policy. But a continually worsening economic climate in the Farm Belt and its potentially ominous repercussions for Republicans in 1986 combined instead to keep the White House and the GOP-controlled Senate on the defensive through most of 1985.

The first piece of farm legislation to come before the Senate that year reflected the basic political hurdle that Farm Belt Republicans would have to overcome throughout the year. At issue was an emergency credit measure cleared in early March that was designed to help debt-ridden farmers through another spring planting season. The administration claimed that the credit bill was nothing more than an unwarranted bailout for bankers who had made unwise loans to farmers during the boom years of agriculture in the 1970s. Railing against the notion of the government once again coming to farmers' rescue was David A. Stockman, director of the White House Office and Management and Budget and Reagan's hatchet man on farm issues. "For the life of me," he told the Senate Budget Committee in February 1985, "I cannot figure out why the taxpayers of this country have the responsibility to go in and refinance bad debt that was willingly incurred by consenting adults."

But farm-state Republicans had a hard time defending that view, particularly after the entire South Dakota legislature flew to Washington in late February to press Congress for more farm benefits. It was an unprecedented and well-televised visit by a predominately Republican group, highlighting intensive lobbying by large contingents from other Midwestern legislatures, including those of North Dakota, Nebraska, and Kansas.

Reagan eventually vetoed the emergency credit bill as too costly, but eight Senate Republicans, by voting for the measure, served early notice that the administration would find few friends for many of its more drastic policy reforms.

Democrats, for their part, took no time in laying claim to farm issues in an effort to show they were more concerned than Republicans about the fate of American farmers. House Agriculture Committee members staged hearings in the spring with movie stars Jane Fonda, Jessica Lange, and Sissy Spacek, on the pretext the latter two had special insights on the issue after appearing in "Country" and "The River," films that evoked a gritty image of family farmers struggling to survive against the twin nemeses of big business and bad weather.

Many Republicans criticized the hearings as blatantly political hype, foisted on Congress by electioneering Democrats. Yet by the end of the summer the political climate surrounding the farm bill debate had gotten so hot that many GOP senators joined their Democratic colleagues in another "media event" with country and rock music recording artists Willie Nelson, Neil Young, and John Conlee, organizers of a benefit concert called "Farm Aid." The musicians came to Capitol Hill to ask senators for "advice" on how to spend the millions of dollars the September 22 concert would raise for destitute farm families.

"No one's talking about how the Farm Aid concert is being politicized," griped a Republican staff member at the time, reflecting a concern among Republican leaders that the farm policy debate had gotten further and further away from their original agenda of fiscal restraint. Members of both parties were drawn into a political cyclone of having to prove the extent of their commitment to farmers. "Sooner or later," complained Kansas Republican Robert Dole, the Senate majority leader, "we're going to have to decide who's the self-appointed protector of the farmer." It was a speech he would make again and again over the next two years.

Not until December 1985 would the farm bill stalemate resolve itself in legislative compromise—a new, five-year reauthorization bill for most of the farm and nutrition programs run by the federal government, and a companion bill to shore up the nation's huge, agricultural lending network known as the Farm Credit System. The White House eventually caved in on many of its ideological points as well as its stated spending limits. Democrats, in turn, had to concede that farm incomes could not be subsidized forever at the existing high rates.

The Aftermath

Even with the hype and political hoopla normally given to agriculture in an election year, Congress hardly tampered in 1986 with the basic tenets of federal farm policy. Continued hard times on the farm had been expected to spur a raft of legislative efforts to reshape, reshuffle, and redesign price- and income-supports. If nothing else, the mere threat of a Democratic takeover of Republican Senate seats in the Farm Belt was supposed to drive the revolt. But the Ninety-ninth Congress adjourned in mid-October with barely a bow to farm groups and legislators who, from all points of the political spectrum, had complained about the alleged inequities of the new farm bill.

Farm exports—the lifeblood of the agricultural economy for the 1970s—failed to pick up measurably from the sharp declines recorded since 1981. Congress tried to rectify the foreign trade problem in the 1985 farm bill by allowing the Reagan administration to drive down the price supports for wheat and corn in an effort to bring them more in line with world market prices. But even with sudden, 40 to 50 percent drops in farm prices in the ensuing year, export sales remained sluggish. Other grain-producing nations, including Argentina, Canada, Australia, and the European Community, continued to undersell U.S. exporters.

In the meantime, however, the Reagan administration managed to silence much of the anticipated outcry for change from farmers. The administration's unbridled use of discretionary spending powers granted by the farm bill sent price- and income-support outlays to unprecedented heights in fiscal 1986, including nearly $13 billion in direct cash payments.

What is more, farmers participated heavily in a new program involving more than $5 billion in government-issued certificates that were being dispersed throughout the country in partial payment of 1986 and early 1987 cash benefits. Farmers could redeem the payment-in-kind (PIK) certificates for the government's massive stocks of surplus food and fiber products, but for a variety of reasons, the "new currency" also took on value as a tradable, money-making commodity. According to many on Capitol Hill, the novelty of the PIK program succeeded in distracting farmers from the problems of the agricultural economy as a whole and from the election-year efforts to remedy the farm bill's perceived shortcomings. "There was no rebellion on the farm this year," said Dan Pearson, an aide to Sen. Rudy Boschwitz, Republican of Minnesota. "There was no rebellion."

Gramm-Rudman Obstacles

A major barrier to nearly every new piece of farm spending legislation was the 1985 Gramm-Rudman-Hollings antideficit law, which effectively required new spending to be neutralized by revenue increases or program cuts elsewhere. The power of Gramm-Rudman over Congress's usual ways of doing business in agriculture was established clearly in 1986, when the Republican-controlled Senate soundly rejected every Democratic proposal to increase benefits to farmers.

One relatively minor measure, which would have increased springtime planting loans to farmers by $1 billion, was billed as the first real test of Gramm-Rudman. And, at first, it looked like the intensifying, election-year pressure on farm-state Republicans would tip the balance of power in the Senate in favor of anti-Gramm-Rudman Democrats. Indeed, ten Republicans from rural states voted for the $1 billion addition in farm loans. But urban Democrats—many of whom had supported Gramm-Rudman to establish their reputations as fiscal conservatives—turned the tables on the farm bloc to vote against the plan,

leading to a surprisingly lopsided, 61-33 vote.

The Gramm-Rudman environment was nonpartisan, however. Senate majority leader Dole, whose role as GOP leader included being protector to the 1980 class of farm-state Senate Republicans, later found himself one of the victims of the new budget-cutting mood. Dole wanted the president and the new secretary of agriculture, Richard E. Lyng, to initiate a new export subsidy program that would include the biggest potential grain buyer in the world, the Soviet Union, among its main beneficiaries. The president's chief foreign affairs, trade, and finance advisers remained firmly opposed to the idea of undercutting staunch international allies (among them struggling holders of U.S. bank loans) with new subsidies. So Dole began drafting legislation to force Reagan's hand.

What stifled his bill, however, was not the foreign policy and international banking community. It was a Congressional Budget Office estimate that his export-incentive program for wheat and feed grains would cost an additional $5 billion in subsidies over the next three years. The facts of political life under Gramm-Rudman meant that Dole had to look for offsetting reductions for his costly bill within the agriculture budget

U.S. farmers produce twice as much food and fiber as the nation can consume. The government buys up much of what cannot be sold overseas and stores it in grain elevators.

itself. Even commodity groups pushing hardest for new export subsidies were unwilling to go along with that notion, afraid to sacrifice the certainty of direct income-support subsidies for the less predictable benefits of a new export-incentive program.

The issue ground down amid back-and-forth negotiations between Dole, farm-group lobbyists, and the administration. In the final two months of the 1986 session, it became a running joke on Capitol Hill as Dole announced daily that he was about to introduce his new legislation—as soon, that is, as he could come up with a "deficit-neutral" package. Dole never introduced a bill.

The Status Quo Prevails

Nineteen eighty-seven began with another Reagan administration assault on basic federal farm policy and a continuing outcry among urban lawmakers over the bloated cost of price-support programs. The year ended with no major changes in farm law.

In between, farm-state lawmakers got absorbed in the nether world of banking and finance when they were confronted with the impending collapse of the nation's largest agricultural lender, the Farm Credit System. Congress spent the better part of the year wrestling with highly technical and complicated legislation to provide a $4 billion bailout for the quasi-private system.

And while all this was happening in Washington, the long-depressed agricultural economy (which had provoked most of the political heartache in the first place) suddenly showed signs of "bottoming out" in both land prices and all-important farm export sales, prompting some policy makers to hail an early resurgence of U.S. agriculture. Often unmentioned in such praise was the fact that nearly a third of farmers' incomes was being provided through government subsidies.

President Reagan kicked off what promised to be another pitched battle with Congress over farm spending. His fiscal 1988 budget essentially created a new Reagan farm policy by calling for an immediate, across-the-board cut in income subsidies to farmers, a proposal that would have required Congress to override the 1985 farm bill and cut target prices for major crops by 10 percent a year, beginning in 1988. Ironically, the administration's decision to attack these key tenets of federal farm policy had the opposite effect of solidifying congressional support for the embattled 1985 farm bill. The new Reagan proposal became the harsh approach, which merely spurred the commercial agriculture community to protect the status quo.

At the opposite extreme from the administration were grass-roots farm groups that had been pushing for more, not less, government intervention in agriculture than provided under the 1985 act. Backed mainly by Midwestern Democrats, this "populist" movement wanted the government to impose strict controls on what a farmer could plant and market as a means of limiting supply and driving up prices. Though unsuccessful in two previous years, supporters of mandatory controls believed their cause was enhanced greatly by 1986 Democratic victories in key farm-state Senate races, where the incumbent Republicans were identified with the existing farm programs.

Congress, under pressure from the administration and from urban liberals to cut costs in agriculture, appeared to have only two choices. One was to cut target prices; the other was to adopt mandatory controls, an option anathema to the administration and most establishment farm groups. But Reagan, by going after target prices to achieve major savings, actually expanded the spectrum of farm policy options. He made a farm bill once identified with Repubicans suddenly look like the middle ground in a Democratic Congress.

The inertia for existing law was strengthened by the distractions created by the impending Farm Credit System crisis and by rumblings of good economic news in the farm belt. U.S. agricultural exports, for example, rose in both value and volume in fiscal 1987 for the first time in nearly a decade, gaining $1.6 billion to $27.9 billion, with forecasts for it to rise to $32 billion or more in 1988. That was still a far cry from the heady days in the late 1970s and early 1980s, when farm exports grew to as much as $44 billion a year. But it represented a big psychological turnaround from the depths of 1985 (when exports plunged to $26.3 billion) for an industry that relied on sales to foreigners for up to 40 percent of its income.

New Global Strategy

In the final analysis, however, the 1985 farm bill remained intact because of an abrupt shift in strategy by the Reagan administration in mid-1987. In July Reagan submitted a proposal to a new round of world trade talks in Geneva, Switzerland, under the auspices of the General Agreement on Tariffs and Trade (GATT), for the complete elimination of farm subsidies by the year 2000. It was the most radical idea on agriculture ever presented to U.S. trading partners, many of whom placed as much, if not more, government resources into agriculture as the United States. But the new Reagan plan demonstrated that the administration had adopted the view of most farm-state lawmakers: that the United States could not afford to change its farm policy unless foreign competitors played along.

However, it was also clear by the middle of 1988 that the complex and often-competing interests of the various countries that subsidize agriculture would make a global agreement no less difficult to achieve than it had been in the U.S. Congress.

Reagan's grand plans for agriculture served mainly to postpone indefinitely the issue of how big a role the government should play in agriculture—and whether it should be involved in agriculture in the first place. No matter what the GATT, Congress, or the new administration does about agriculture in 1989 and beyond, their actions will be built upon a foundation of farm laws and concepts already rooted in generations of previous economic and political experience. This is true about all facets of government, of course, but especially so in agriculture.

There are, quite literally, no new ideas in farm policy. Anything that will be done has been done. Or tried.

Chapter 2

Price-Support Programs

The problem is a corn farmer in Indiana, name of Luck.

For most of the sixty-seven years he had been living in north central Indiana, raising feedcorn, soybeans, and even a little popcorn on an eight-hundred-acre, family-owned spread, Harold W. Luck had little use for federal farm programs. He hated the idea of them. They brought the kind of government interference that no "self-respecting" farmer in his part of the country would stand for. So Luck would say no thanks to federal handouts. "I've never taken the government support in my life," the White County native said in early 1987. "If I can't make a profit on my operations, I can't see what the government can do to help me."

But then Luck, like many of his neighbors, had been used to making a living on his own. His part of Indiana is blessed with black, mineral-rich soil, which made feedcorn cheap and easy to produce year after year. Farming was actually a consistently profitable enterprise in that corner of the Farm Belt. Back in 1982 the average cash income for Indiana farmers was close to the national average of $60,000—yet the typical Indiana farmer got about half as much from the government as farmers in the rest of the country. (See Figure 2-1.)

Politically the state is a bastion of antigovernment sentiment, a Republican free-market stronghold. The independent-minded farmers of Indiana just do not want to "mess with the paperwork" that comes with U.S. farm price-support programs. Luck fit the mold. "I'm pretty well market-oriented," he liked to say. "Let supply and demand dictate."

So why did this proud, independent, successful corn farmer

Figure 2-1 Selected Farming Subregions

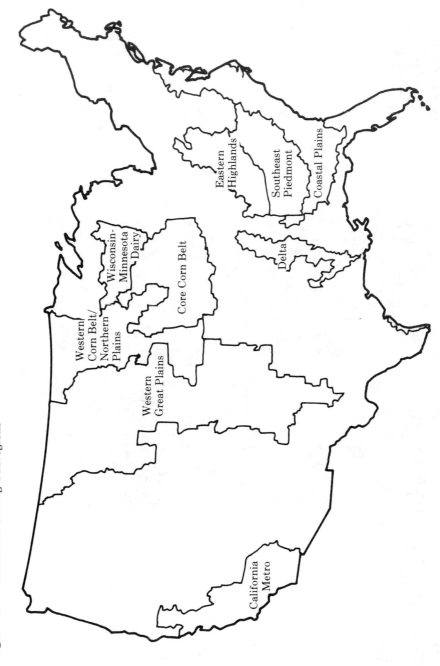

Source: U.S. Department of Agriculture, Economic Research Service, Agriculture and Rural Economy Division, *Regional Characteristics of U.S. Farms and Farmers in the 1980s*, prepared by Matthew G. Smith and Fred Hines (Washington, D.C.: Government Printing Office, 1988), 6-7.

Note: The Wisconsin-Minnesota Dairy subregion, a belt running across the middle of Wisconsin into central Minnesota, relies heavily on dairy sales and has a relatively low proportion of production from large farms and low rates of nonfarm jobholding. As a result, the farm population of the region heavily depends on income from farming.

The Core Corn Belt, extending from northern Illinois to eastern Nebraska and from northern Missouri to southern Minnesota, relies heavily on sales of program crops and has a low proportion of part-time operators. The region depends heavily on farm income, and farmers make up a relatively high proportion of the rural population.

The Delta subregion extends from southeastern Missouri to Louisiana. It depends more than any subregion on sales of program crops, which provided 85 percent of gross farm income in 1982. It has a low proportion of farm operators working full time off the farm.

The Eastern Highlands subregion, running from southeastern Ohio through the Appalachians into central Tennessee, has very low sales per farm and a very high percentage of total sales from small farms. Farm operators have a greater tendency to work full time off the farm, and the farm population has a high rate of nonfarm jobholding.

The Western Great Plains extends from West Texas to the Canadian border west of the Missouri River. It has a very high average farm size in acreage, and low rates of part-time farming and nonfarm jobholding. The farm population depends heavily on farming for its income.

The Western Corn Belt/Northern Plains run from northern Kansas to North Dakota, with a spur running down through western Minnesota and north-central Iowa. It has very low rates of part-time farming and nonfarm jobholding and relies more than any region on farming as a source of income. Farmers also make up the largest proportion by far of the total rural population (nearly a third).

The Coastal Plains of the Atlantic seaboard extend from the southern tip of New Jersey to northern Florida and back up to east-central Mississippi. In many respects, it reflects the U.S. average. It relies somewhat more heavily on sales of program crops and less on dairy sales and has a slightly higher rate of nonfarm jobholding and a lower dependence on farm income.

The Southeast Piedmont, from North Carolina to northern Georgia, relies less than other areas on sales of either program crops or dairy products. It has the highest proportion of operators with full-time off-farm jobs and a high rate of nonfarm employment by the farm population. Farming supplies a below-average share of total farm household income.

The California Metro subregion consists of the southern, midcoastal, and central valley areas of California. It relies heavily on sales of nonprogram crops and has a very large average farm size and a high proportion of sales from large farms.

take a check from the U.S. Treasury for $23,428 in 1986, and
another one for $16,631 in 1987? And why did he plan to enlist
for more in 1988 and future years? What happened to his free-
market philosophy, his aversion to government help? How did
he justify the double standard?

Well, that's simple, said Luck: "It's economic necessity."

Like it or not, Harold Luck and his neighbors were stuck in
a double bind of modern agriculture. It forced these conservative business people to rely on government subsidies like never
before. Luck, growing more corn than ever, was suddenly unable
to sell his crops at a break-even price, certainly not for a price
better than the government would pay him. Where he once
found ready buyers for his corn at $3.50 to $4.00 a bushel—well
above the old government support price of $3.30—Luck in
recent years had trouble unloading his produce at even $1.50 a
bushel. In 1986 Uncle Sam took the corn off his hands for $2.16,
then gave him another $1.50 as a "deficiency payment" to make
up for the lost income. As much as he disliked the implications,
Luck said, it was an offer he could not refuse.

Now he is an annual enrollee in what most farmers refer to
simply as "the program." "It would be really unreasonable to
raise corn out here without taking what they're offering," he
explained. "There's no way I could survive without being in the
program. It's break even or a little above until I get my government help. That payment is going to make the profit for me."

This is the modern farmer's dilemma: an avowed distaste,
yet profound need, for government aid. It was a condition
shared by thousands of corn farmers in Indiana and other
productive regions of the Corn Belt, and during the mid-1980s it
became the untold story of U.S. agriculture. The emergence of
farmers like Harold Luck as dependents of federal farm price
supports was the main reason the government spent a record
$26 billion in fiscal 1986 and $21 billion in fiscal 1987 to stabilize prices and the incomes of farmers. The record expenditures
occurred only six years after the government's farm tab came in
at less than $4 billion—at that time the high end of what farm
programs were supposed to cost through the rest of the decade.

Jumping on the Bandwagon

As federal price-support programs approach their seventh
decade of propping up the U.S. agricultural economy, the costs

of running them have begun to overwhelm the continuing debate over what is the most effective governmental farm policy. The questions of how and why the government should get involved in farming have been eclipsed by a more pressing political crisis—namely, cutting a ballooning federal budget deficit, which grew from $40 billion in 1981 to a mammoth $221 billion 1986.

But the volatile budget debate, while exposing agriculture spending to intense political scrutiny in Washington, only clouded the true financial relationship between farmer and government. As public attention began to focus on the $20 billion allocated for farm programs in the federal budget, an important transformation was taking place within the programs themselves.

Government support has taken command of agricultural production decisions in the United States. For both crop prices and farmer incomes, federal subsidies now play the dominant role in determining how much of certain commodities will be produced and what prices they will bring at the market. In 1980, government outlays for corn, wheat, and rice represented less than 7 percent of the total value of those crops. This share grew to about 57 percent by 1986 and in the case of rice, which experienced a massive decline in prices as a result of overproduction, government outlays actually exceeded the value of the crop. Government income subsidies to farmers, which accounted for only 4 percent of net farm income in 1980, rose to 23 percent in 1986. By 1988, after experiencing some of their worst financial times in agriculture since the Great Depression, farmers found that their circumstances were improving in many ways, but practically all of the gains were a direct result of increased government aid. (See Table 2-1.)

As farmers came to depend more and more on government benefits to get by, their attitudes toward farm programs began to change as well. Indiana corn farmers were a case in point. In 1982, when farm programs cost a then-unprecedented $12 billion, only one in five Indiana corn farmers signed up for federal benefits. Most figured rightly that they could get by with selling their crops on the open market. Only those with little business savvy or others in the most desperate financial straits would enroll their corn in the program. In Indiana, taking money from the federal government was a sign of poor farm management or, worse, socialistic political tendencies.

Table 2-1   Direct Subsidies to Corn Farmers as Percentage of U.S. Corn Production Value

	1977	1978	1979	1980	1981	1982	1983	1984	1985	1986	1987
Farm value of production (in billions)	$13.1	$16.3	$19.9	$20.6	$20.2	$22.0	$19.2	$20.1	$21.3	$12.3	$11.9
Direct government payments (in billions)	$0.3	$0.7	$0.1	$0.3	$0.1	$0.3	$0.9	$1.8	$2.7	$6.4	$8.2
Government payments as percentage of corn production value	2	4	0.5	1	0.5	1	5	9	13	52	69

Source: U.S. Department of Agriculture.

In 1987, however, more than half of the 114,000 corn operations in Indiana were enrolled in federal price-support programs, representing 83 percent of the land devoted to corn in that state. That meant that four out of every five bushels produced in one of the country's most profitable corn-growing regions were protected by federal price and income supports.

In many cases, the decision to enter the program was not a farmer's alone. Farm programs in the mid-1980s became the money-back guarantee that many agricultural bankers required before they would lend money to farmers for buying land or planting new crops. "It's almost to the point where it's mandatory for a farmer to be in the program," said Larry Riggs, branch manager of Farm Credit System's local production credit and land bank associations in Anderson, Ind. "For a lender to loan money today, we almost have to make a commitment based on [the farmer's] involvement in the program. It just doesn't work if he's not there."

Across the nation, corn farmers and their bankers responded in much the same way. Where only 29 percent of the corn acreage "base" in the United States was protected by federal price-support programs in 1982, nearly 88 percent was covered in 1987. Farmers throughout the Midwest Corn Belt were jumping on the bandwagon. (See Figure 2-2.)

Wheat farmers, in contrast, were always more inclined to take part in government programs, if for no other reason than most of them are located in the high plains states, where only wheat is growable. Unlike most Midwestern corn growers, they cannot switch to soybeans or other commodities if the market

Figure 2-2   Farm Program Participation

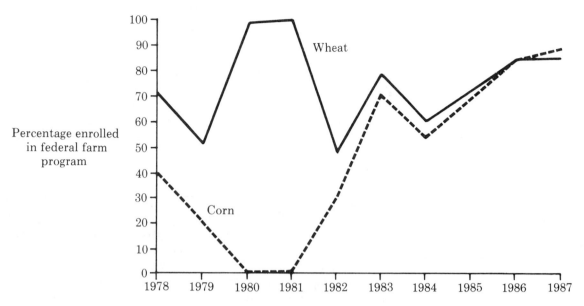

Source: U.S. Department of Agriculture.

demand for their principle staple dries up. Wheat crops also are easily ruined by hail, wind, and other natural disturbances. As a result, wheat farmers seeking protection from the government have enrolled an average of 60 percent of their acres in the federal wheat program since 1981, with participation never dropping below 48 percent.

Yet by 1986, even wheat farmers began running in record numbers for the government's protective cover. The participation rate for wheat climbed to 84 percent in 1986 and was expected to remain at that level before dipping back down to the 75 percent range in the early 1990s.

The blow to taxpayers from this wave of interest in federal price-support programs—particularly by corn farmers—was staggering. The cost of running just the corn programs went from $4.3 billion in fiscal 1982 to $10.4 billion in fiscal 1986, rising even further to $12.3 billion in fiscal 1987. The increase accounted for 44 percent of the $14.2 billion jump in spending for all farm programs between 1982 and 1986. (See Table 2-2.)

The cost of wheat and other commodity programs also went up, though at far lower levels. The wheat program cost $2.8

billion in fiscal 1987, up from $2.2 billion in fiscal 1982. Cotton program expenditures rose from $1.2 billion to $2.1 billion. Rice went from $163,000 to nearly $1 billion.

Projections for wheat, cotton, and rice programs actually showed some significant cost reductions in 1988 and beyond. According to the Congressional Budget Office (CBO), however, the uncertain market outlook for corn virtually ensured that 85 percent of all corn acres would remain under federal price and income supports through 1991. That could only mean the cost of the corn program would stay near current levels; CBO predicted that by fiscal 1991, outlays for corn would still be nearly $10 billion.

The Price-Support System

For more than fifty years, the broad objective of farm programs has been to absorb the risk farmers incur from wildly fluctuating prices for commodities, which trade in the most volatile markets in the world. Since World War II, U.S. farm policy has centered on price stabilization and crop insurance schemes designed to help farmers cope with ever-changing physical and economic climates. These programs deal mainly with corn, wheat, cotton, and rice, which together with soybeans occupy three of every four commercially planted acres of land in the United States. Farm price-support programs are based on this simple premise: the entire crop sector of the country can be

Table 2-2 Corn and Wheat Program Outlays

	1977	1978	1979	1980	1981	1982	1983	1984	1985	1986	1987
Corn outlays (in billions)	$0.40	$1.70	$0.87	$1.26	$−0.67	$4.28	$5.72	$−0.93	$4.40	$10.52	$12.05
Corn outlays as percentage of total farm programs	11	30	19	46	0	37	30	22	25	41	54
Wheat outlays (in billions)	$1.90	$0.84	$0.31	$0.88	$1.54	$2.24	$3.42	$2.54	$4.69	$3.44	$ 2.84
Wheat outlays as percentage of total farm programs	50	15	9	32	38	19	18	35	27	13	13

Source: U.S. Department of Agriculture.

Note: Fiscal years.

managed if these crops can be managed.

Over the years, a two-tier system has evolved to perform the federal government's imposing task. The first tier entails the government's unflagging commitment to buy farmers' products at a certain price if they cannot sell them for at least that much on the open market. At harvestime, the Agriculture Department offers low-interest loans to farmers who agree to hold all or part of their crops off the market for as long as nine months. The goal is to spread sales over the course of a full marketing year and prevent a glut (and depressed prices) during the brief period of time when most farmers bring their crops in from the fields.

Congress sets the rate for this price-support "loan." It is done on a bushel basis, requiring the Agriculture Department to offer a farmer, say, $2.00 a bushel for corn, with the farmer putting up the crop itself as collateral. The government takes control of the crop at harvestime, and if at the end of the nine-month term the farmer-borrower has not been able to get a market price that is better than the loan rate, the farmer can forfeit the entire crop to the government and keep the principal—that is, the original $2.00 a bushel. Other than taking over the crop, the government has no other recourse to get its money back. Farmers come under no penalty for nonpayment of the loan. They do not suffer any stigma either; nothing like a bad credit rating attaches to a farmer who defaults on a price-support loan. These are "nonrecourse" loans. In effect, the government buys the crop at $2.00 a bushel, guaranteeing the farmer who participates in the program at least that much when signing up at the beginning of the year.

More importantly, under this scheme the government becomes the residual buyer for all surplus production of a particular commodity. In practice, the marketplace determines the price of a commodity based on available supply. The more corn there is available, compared with a normally stable demand, the lower the price. But if the government is buying up so much corn or wheat at predetermined prices, it automatically absorbs whatever amount of grain exceeds real market demand. It artificially shorts the market and drives prices upward. The loan rate becomes an effective floor on prices for all farmers, whether they actually participate in the program or not.

For years farmers like Harold Luck got the benefit of prices jacked up by government supports, even when they were not

Government farm programs have become so essential to making a profit that many bankers will not make loans to farmers unless they first sign up for federal price and income guarantees. Here a management specialist helps a Nebraska farmer analyze his cash flow to see how much he will need to borrow.

enrolled in the program. As long as the government was buying up corn at $2.50 a bushel, and as long as prices for all farmers stayed at that level or higher, Indiana farmers and others who enjoyed generally lower production costs than their counterparts in less fertile regions of the country could reap the windfall. They got the advantage both ways. Without having anything to do with the program, their crops were protected by the artificial prices the program created.

On top of price supports, Congress in the 1970s also began to set ideal "target" prices for each crop, reflecting its notion of the ideal return for a farmer. This income-support program was

36

instituted at a time when actual market prices were higher than the targets. If prices fell, the government would be obligated to give participating farmers a "deficiency" payment to cover the shortfall between the target price and either the price received for that crop or the loan rate, whichever was higher. It was designed to cushion the blow of lower prices.

A key feature of these price- and income-support programs, as far as the government is concerned, is the ability to control production from year to year. In years of expected surpluses, the government periodically made farmers reduce their planted acreage as a prerequisite for getting direct government supports. The government became the arbiter of supply and prices.

The Export Boom

For a variety of reasons, including the effect of the government's direct involvement in the farm economy, market prices for the major commodities stayed well above both loan rates and target prices through much of the inflationary 1970s. President Richard Nixon's grain agreement with the Soviet Union kicked off an era of heavy export demand for wheat and feed grains. The fall in value of the U.S. dollar in the early 1970s and the positive effects of low interest rates, relative to inflation, through the rest of the decade stimulated big increases in farm production. By 1980, more than one-third of U.S. crop land was committed to producing for export.

The government was still buying some grain during this period, mainly to hold enough off the market to keep market prices above target prices. As long as market prices stayed above the targets, government costs for farm programs remained minimal. Few farmers forfeited their crops, and deficiency payments rarely came into play.

But during this time of rising exports and dwindling surpluses, it became politically expedient to raise loan rates and target prices. Congress, spurred by both the Ford and Carter administrations, made points with farmers by raising support prices even though market prices were still keeping well ahead. "Everyone said, 'Let's increase price supports when it won't cost us anything,'" recalled one House Agriculture Committee aide. "It didn't cost anything, but it built the floor on which everything has been added since. What it didn't cost us in the 1970s, it is costing us now."

The Bubble Bursts

Then, in a complete reversal of policy, the government in 1985 decided to pull the rug out from under commodity prices in a risky attempt to pump new life into a slumping agriculture economy.

In the early 1980s, the single biggest force that spurred prosperity for U.S. farmers—the export market—had begun to dry up. Farm sales overseas plummeted to $26 billion in 1986 after reaching a pinnacle of $44 billion in 1981. U.S. farmers, however, kept producing bumper crops as if the market were still thriving. And in a strange sense it was. The 1981 farm bill established loan rates and target prices on an upward scale to reflect the double-digit inflation that characterized the economy at the time. It was widely assumed that inflation, which averaged 13.5 percent in 1980, would continue to outpace an increase in target prices of "merely" 6 percent a year.

But inflation slowed and world prices suddenly turned downward. Large grain-producing nations such as Argentina, Brazil, Australia, and Canada pushed their farmers to step up grain exports when it became apparent they could undersell U.S. products and still make hefty profits. European farmers, using blatantly predatory Common Market subsidies, pumped up their grain factories to become the United States' biggest competitor instead of its biggest market. Meanwhile, agricultural skill increased in many developing countries, allowing them to grow their own grain instead of having to buy expensive U.S. crops.

American farmers, who had become dependent on export sales for much of their sales, were left with few alternatives other than to forfeit most of their crops to the government. More and more farmers began to sign up for government programs, and as a result, farm program costs went skyward. And as the government bought up increasing amounts of grain stocks, the Reagan administration began to implement larger and larger acreage reduction programs in an effort to hold down the cost of providing income subsidies on the bushels produced under the program.

In 1983, the supply-management theory behind the government's price-support programs reached its zenith. The Agriculture Department instituted a massive acreage reduction program, enticing farmers with offers of government-owned grain if they agreed to cut back up to 100 percent of their normal production. The 1983 payment-in-kind (PIK) program idled more crop land in the United States than all of Western Europe planted that year. Combined with a drought in the Corn Belt, the PIK program helped drive down corn production to 4.1 billion bushels, from 8.2 billion bushels the year before. All of a sudden, an administration that had come to power spouting a free-market economic philosophy became the main proponent of one of the most interventionist policies in the history of agriculture.

Agriculture Department officials were nonetheless pleased at how the PIK program reduced government surpluses, and they ordered only a modest acreage reduction program in 1984. The White House also pulled back from its previous efforts to eliminate target prices, agreeing to a compromise with Congress that reduced loan rates slightly but kept target prices on their upward scale for one additional year.

But after enticing so many farmers into the PIK program, the department suddenly experienced a sharp increase in enrollments for the normal 1984 program. As corn production rebounded to 7.6 billion bushels nationwide, more than half of the corn acreage in the country was covered by price and income supports. "Farmers learned to take advantage of the program," said David Hull, a corn-program analyst at the Agriculture Department's Economic Research Service. "The 1983 PIK program was the turning point. Farmers who didn't take part kicked themselves when they saw what their neighbors were getting."

A record corn crop of 8.8 billion bushels in 1985, combined with a 70 percent participation rate among corn farmers, sealed the fate of the program. The record $25.6 billion in farm program outlays in fiscal 1986 would be largely a reflection of program costs incurred during the 1985 crop year.

The 1985 Farm Bill

Already conscious of rising costs and scared of the doomsday predictions that could be coming true, Congress and the Reagan administration in 1985 responded with unusual consensus on basic price-support policy: support prices had to come down. At the same time, concerns in Congress over the cost of subsidizing farm exports, coupled with the record cost of farm

The modern farmer's dilemma: an avowed distaste, yet profound need, for government aid.

price supports in the early 1980s, only added to the difficulties of writing a new omnibus farm bill that followed the government's deficit-reduction agenda.

Ultimately, what had started in the Reagan White House as an anxious desire for wholesale changes in the way the government propped up farm production gave way in Congress to nervous anxiety over the consequences for farmers. A fragile coalition of the competing interests that characterized the agriculture community began falling in step behind the banner of boosting exports. But lobbyists, exporters, and farmers remained divided on how best to win back foreign markets for U.S.-grown products.

The emphasis on export subsidies and the controversies surrounding them, however, only served to weaken the incentive in Congress to make sweeping reforms in price-support policy. The administration wanted to set loan rates at 75 percent of average market prices, a radical departure from existing law that led even Republican farm-state legislators to call the administration proposals to Congress "dead on arrival."

Democratic House leaders—in particular, Majority Whip Thomas S. Foley, former chairman of the Agriculture Committee and, at the time of the farm bill debate, chairman of the pivotal Subcommittee on Wheat, Soybeans and Feed Grains—were willing to restructure loan rates to keep them more attuned to market fluctuations. But they insisted on only modest reductions.

Congress eventually crafted a new farm programs authorization bill that promised to cut loan rates sharply in 1986. The rates would be determined by a new market-oriented formula, one pegged to the price those crops would actually bring at the market instead of the cost of producing them. Corn price supports, for instance, were slashed from $2.55 a bushel in 1985 to $1.92 a bushel in 1986, and the five-year farm bill also authorized the agriculture secretary to drive loan rates down another 5 percent each year through 1990, when they could go as low as $1.56 a bushel—a ninety-nine-cent decline over the life of the legislation.

The stated hope was that lower price supports would bring U.S. prices down to existing world levels and allow farmers to win back foreign customers for their grain. To some extent, it worked. But the political trade-off for that policy was costly, and promised to be for some time to come.

John R. Block was President Reagan's first agriculture secretary and the main spokesman for the administration's unsuccessful efforts to scale back the government's costly involvement in agriculture.

To win Congress's approval for reducing price supports, the administration had to go along with the demands of powerful farm-state members to bolster farmers' incomes in other ways. First they hearkened on exports—subsidizing them as well as creating more markets for them—as the main way to increase sales and reduce farmer dependency on the government price supports. Seizing on the fact that the European Economic Community had been using export subsidies to win away many of the markets that American farmers' had come to depend on, Farm Belt senators pushed for the same kinds of government subsidies to help put U.S. traders back on an even footing with foreign competitors.

During the bitter 1985 budget battle in the Senate, several farm-state senators had forced a reluctant Reagan administration to agree to implement a controversial export "enhancement" program in exchange for their support of the Reagan-backed deficit-reduction plan. Agriculture secretary John R. Block, in hopes of forestalling congressional action that would mandate an even more wide-ranging export subsidy scheme, initiated a program to give away $2 billion worth of government-owned commodities in a few selected markets where U.S. exporters had lost customers as a result of predatory European subsidies.

Farm-state lawmakers also fought to keep target prices at the previous high levels. In fact, whether to freeze target prices or begin to cut them became the focal point of the entire 1985 farm bill debate. The administration and conservative Republicans pressed for immediate reductions in target prices. Democrats and farm-state Republicans, on the other hand, wanted to freeze target prices at 1985 levels through the life of the bill.

The target-price issue wrapped the Senate in a protracted, partisan tangle that was not unsnarled until late in the year. The final farm bill, signed by Reagan December 23, 1985, contained a standard compromise by effectively splitting the difference. It froze target prices for wheat and corn in 1986 and 1987 and permitted annual reductions of only 2 percent, 3 percent, and 5 percent for the remaining three years under the bill.

Reagan's ultimate blessing for the 1985 farm bill brought a tense standoff between the White House and Congress to a classic "win-win" conclusion: The results pleased few in Congress or the administration, but, more important politically, they angered fewer. The administration, which had fought since

Majority Leader Thomas S. Foley, D-Wash., moved up the ranks of the House leadership through the Agriculture Committee, where he served as chairman of the full panel and of the pivotal Subcommittee on Wheat, Soybeans and Feed Grains.

1981 to cut the tether that binds farmers and the federal government, won a bill that immediately lowered basic price supports and promised to reduce annual federal outlays for agriculture by half. But an election-conscious Congress, swayed by powerful sentiment for struggling "family farmers," won a bill that subsidized farmers' incomes at record levels for at least three more years, and two congressional elections. "The truth is," summed up one Democratic leader, "we got the money, and the [administration] got a little bit of principle."

Paying the Price

From that elemental policy battle, however, ensued a fundamental shift in farm program spending, one that will certainly become the point of political conflict between Congress and the White House, and between urban and rural interests, for the next decade.

In the first place, the sharp reductions in price-support loan rates in 1986 had the unintended effect of forcing even more farmers than usual to turn their 1985 crops over to the government. Consider again the 1985 corn crop. It was protected by a loan rate of $2.55 per bushel. When the administration announced that the 1986 loan rate would be dropped to $1.92, the market responded immediately. Prices plummeted. Farmers with 1985 corn still "under loan" at $2.55 per bushel had little chance to get a better price on the market, so they forfeited their grain to the government. As a result, net lending for the corn program—the difference between loans made in one year and loans repaid from the previous year, plus storage and handling costs—went from $1.8 billion in fiscal 1985 to an estimated $8.2 billion in fiscal 1987.

Secondly, even though the target price for corn was frozen at $3.03 per bushel, deficiency payments actually increased as a result of the decline in loan rates and market prices. The average forty-eight-cents-a-bushel deficiency payment in 1985 jumped to $1.11 in 1986, and was expected to rise to $1.21 in 1987, $1.15 in 1988, and $1.17 in 1989 before it begins to trickle back downward. So even though loan forfeitures were expected to decrease significantly in 1988, as loan rates came more into line with actual market prices, the government would nonetheless be making up the difference in direct income subsidies.

One manifestation of the switch in emphasis was the emergence of farmers like Harold Luck as primary beneficiaries of the program. Where Luck's crop was once indirectly protected by government price supports no matter whether he actually enrolled in the program, he now had to enter the program to reap the more-significant income subsidies. Kent Yeager, who grows corn in southern Indiana, faced the same predicament. Like Luck, Yeager and his neighbors swallowed their pride and jumped on board the program. "It's not a situation that most of us farmers want to be in," Yeager said. "We don't like getting money from the government. But you've got to be almost independently wealthy not to participate."

Consequently, a climate of political fatalism came to permeate the agriculture community as their representatives in Congress grappled with the frustrating reality of runaway farm program costs. "Almost without saying so, it's obvious this country's going to have land reform," said George Likens, another Indiana corn farmer. "The government is not going to keep sending all this money out to farmers."

"The problem is, this country's full of corn now," added Harold Luck. "If you wanted any sympathy for this farm program, you've called the wrong man."

Chapter 3

The 'Farm Question'

The marriage of farmer and government dates back some seventy-five years, to when Congress first got the idea that taxpayer funds should go to the aid of agriculture. At the time, farmers wanted their political representatives to add a measure of price stability and income security to the highly unpredictable swings in the farm economy. The fact that farmers and rural citizens, whose livelihoods revolved around the agricultural economy, made up nearly half of the population in the 1920s only enhanced their standing in Washington. From the beginning agriculture policy in the United States was built as much on political foundations as economic ones.

Over the years successive Congresses and presidents found a variety of ways to comfort and protect this important political constituency. Their overtures came mainly in the forms of debt relief and price protection—more money pumped into the fledgling Federal Land Banks, more gimmicks to help farmers get better prices for their crops.

All the while, however, politicians insisted their intervention into the agricultural economy represented only short-term fixes. In 1934 agriculture secretary Henry A. Wallace made a point to insist that federal efforts to manage the farm economy were just "a temporary method for dealing with an emergency." His words echoed through two generations of political decision making. The agricultural policies enacted during those years have been changed from time to time, but for the most part, the original goals and legislative provisions are still recognizable in the farm programs of today.

Yet it has only been lately—since the pivotal year of 1972—

Henry A. Wallace, agriculture secretary during the 1930s under President Roosevelt, was the architect of the "temporary" price-support policies that have remained in force for more than fifty years.

45

that the romance between Congress and an ever-dwindling number of farmers has become fixed, immutable, and probably everlasting. In the fifteen or so years since then, American farmers have passed through some of their best times in history, and U.S. agriculture, an industry once geared mainly to domestic consumption, has become a productive supplier of food and fiber throughout the world.

But U.S. taxpayers, in the meantime, have lost some important assurances: that the farm economy would behave in predictable ways; that farmers would be guaranteed a modest, regular return from the land; that the government's cost of providing the guarantee would stay within modest, affordable bounds. Farmers in the late 1980s instead suffered some of their worst times since the Great Depression, even while the price tag of federal subsidies rose to nearly ten times their cost only a decade before.

Farm spending is an "accident waiting to happen," in the words of Gordon Rausser, a University of California at Berkeley agricultural economist who served with President Reagan's Council of Economic Advisers in 1987. "Somewhere along the line it's going to have to come unraveled," he predicted.

Where did it all go wrong? One place to put the blame could be on the Soviet Union, since that government entered the world grain market in 1972 and immediately rewrote the rules of global trade in agriculture with its massive purchases. Or, one could simply fault the past generation of American politicians—Republicans and Democrats alike—for falling over each other in a Keystone Koplike race to be the self-appointed protectors of the embattled family farmer. Better yet, lay it on Richard Nixon: He took the United States off fixed currency exchange rates and threw commodity markets into a spin from which they have never unwound.

Together these various culprits helped to create such a maze of erratic market attitudes, overbearing farm laws, and completely self-serving political choices that it should not be surprising that U.S. farmers have turned into helpless victims. They are the ones who must live and work under the terms of a confusing, crazy-quilt patchwork of programs and policies, which rule this nation's agricultural economy and probably the rest of the world's, too.

In the end, it is impossible to fix the blame on any one person or event. Because U.S. farm policy is ultimately a prod-

uct of the political system, it is by definition a series of carefully crafted compromises between often polar points of view. Because it tries to impose legal order on rather poorly understood and essentially anarchic rules of the marketplace, farm law will often create as many problems as it solves.

U.S. farm policy tries to predict what is the most unpredictable phenomenon—the weather. Pictured is a dust storm that took place in Cimarron County, Okla., in 1936.

And because it also tries to predict what is, at bottom, the most unpredictable phenomenon—the weather—farm programs are probably a lost cause to begin with. For example, in 1972, the same year that Nixon opened the gates to the Soviet Union and shuffled the rules of currency exchange, unleashing a new era of world agricultural trade, yet another interloper stepped into the scene. It carried the harmless-sounding name of El Niño—"The Child"—but it would eventually wreak havoc on agriculture and practically all attempts by the U.S. government to control it.

El Niño is a mysterious ocean current that appears every six or seven years (usually around Christmastime, hence its name) in the equatorial reefs of South America. It is a wonder of nature that seems always to be disturbing the natural—or rather, habitual—order of things. In 1987 it caused a two-monthlong drought in the rainiest region of the United States, the Pacific Northwest. Other years it turned all kinds of marine and agricultural production cycles topsy turvy. In 1972 El Niño merely made the anchovies disappear from the coast of Peru, but the result was a classic example of how governments must rush to the rescue when farmers are caught short by unexpected (and unexplained) events of nature. The rippling effects of that 1972 episode on the agricultural economy and on U.S. farm policy could still be felt more than fifteen year years later.

Central Questions

How—and why—the relationship between farmer and government got started are questions central to a running political battle in Congress. The battle goes beyond the issue of how much is currently being spent on federal farm programs. That is largely the result of more and more farmers (particularly corn farmers) choosing to take part in programs that prop up food prices and farm income.

A more fundamental question is why so many farmers feel compelled to seek protection from the government. The answers to all of these questions, elusive to rural and nonrural lawmakers alike, get more complicated when considered in light of an additional factor dominating all congressional action in the late 1980s: reducing the federal deficit.

Only in relatively recent years have the House and Senate Agriculture committees responsible for basic farm policy begun taking stock of the cost of programs under their jurisdiction. Some say they have yet to come to grips with it. Many urban lawmakers, in particular, view the record amounts spent on farm programs as a big pot of money that could be better used elsewhere.

Yet within the agricultural community, at least, the battle lines have been drawn for generations. The question, posed at the extremes, comes down to whether U.S. agriculture is better served by shrinking to meet only domestic demand or by expanding to meet world demand. The solutions, also posed at the extremes, would put grain farmers under the firm control of the government or else release them completely into the so-called free market.

Lawmakers and agriculture experts have haggled over this "farm question" since well before 1933, when Congress enacted the first major acreage-reduction program and laid the cornerstone of the basic price-support structure that still exists. Oddly, the debate has been remarkably static. As ever, the

Nineteen eighty-eight Democratic presidential hopeful Richard A. Gephardt, D-Mo., advocated letting farmers vote on whether to impose mandatory acreage controls on wheat and corn production, a policy designed to cut production and raise commodity prices.

arguments involve such somnolent economic precepts as elasticity and market-clearing equilibrium, as well as fundamental political and social ideals such as free market and family farm.

To put it bluntly, there are no new ideas in farm policy. From the Reagan administration's attempts to force farmers back into the free market, to the most radical Democratic plan to impose nationwide control over grain production, the "interminable postwar farm dialogue" (as it was described by one observer as long ago as 1963) continues to seesaw between the two opposing philosophies.

The Reagan administration's proposal in 1987 to decouple farm program benefits by removing payments from a direct relationship to crop production is a good example of how timeless the debate can be. At its core, "decoupling" is an attempt to encourage farmers to make planting decisions in response to real demands. Reagan administration theorists believed that farmers grow certain commodities for the promise of government subsidies even when there is no market for their crops.

Yet similar market-oriented payment schemes were advocated in the earliest years of farm programs. A system of market manipulation prevailed, however, on the theory that if the government could force prices up, direct income subsidies (which decoupling requires as an offset to reduced prices) would be unnecessary.

Another throwback is the drive among populist Midwestern farm groups to let farmers themselves vote on whether to impose mandatory acreage controls on wheat and corn production. This idea was promoted heavily in Iowa and other important presidential primary states by 1988 Democratic presidential aspirants Richard A. Gephardt and Jesse Jackson and, for a time, Gary Hart and Joseph R. Biden, Jr., among others. Yet far from being a "new idea" for agriculture, mandatory acreage controls formed the centerpiece of the 1962 farm programs authorization bill pushed through Congress by President John F. Kennedy. His proposal, moreover, was simply a stricter version of the "supply management" policies that had governed agriculture since 1941.

"If an agricultural policy observer awoke today from a 25-year coma, he or she would feel they have missed little," Martin Abel, a Washington-based agricultural economist and consultant, noted in 1987. "The more things change, the more they stay the same."

Export Driven

If the terms of the debate have not changed, however, the economic realities that could determine each side's relevance—and validity—have altered dramatically.

Before 1972, the government had maintained a close, protective role in agriculture, providing subsidies and other price-support programs mainly to ensure farmers against the vagaries of weather and price. Before 1972, farm policy sought reasonable and stable food prices, gradually expanded exports, and relatively low federal outlays.

That year, however, U.S. farmers revved up for a new era of export-driven production. The fall in value of the U.S. dollar, new trade opportunities throughout the world, and, most important, the emergence of the Soviet Union as a big buyer in the international grain market pushed crop prices and farm incomes to record levels.

Using new farming techniques and technologies, made affordable by rising crop prices, farmers expanded their output to unprecedented levels. Wheat production jumped from 1.4 billion bushels in 1970 to 2.4 billion in 1980. Corn output went from 4.1 billion bushels in 1972 to 6.6 billion ten years later. By 1980 more than one-third of U.S. crop land was committed to producing for export, and two out of every five tons of farm products traded in the world were produced in the United States.

It appeared, for a brief time, that farmers could survive without government protection. It was hoped the new prosperity in farm country would finally close out an arrangement that began in 1933—but that actually dated from 1922, when Congress first tried to put a safety net under the farm economy with legislation to establish price and income supports. (President Calvin Coolidge vetoed that and other interventionist farm bills, forcing Congress to wait until Franklin D. Roosevelt took office to enact the precursors of existing support programs.)

But other events in 1972 made complete divorce impossible. For various reasons, Congress and the Nixon administration jumped in the fray with a desperate effort to control a runaway situation. Their unlikely intervention in the agricultural economy would presage a trend of governmental action that, over the next fifteen years, would force taxpayers time and again to come to the rescue of farmers whenever they called for help.

The Turning Point

In the summer of 1972, President Nixon and his secretary of agriculture, Earl Butz, had just wrapped up a historic grain purchase agreement with the Soviet Union. As part of the deal, the Soviets promised to buy nearly every extra bushel of corn and feed grain that U.S. farmers could produce. The agreement promised to rid the government of a growing surplus problem, plus put an aging body of farm laws in its grave. An exuberant Butz boasted that farmers would at last be free of the "yoke of bureaucratic control." (See Figure 3-1.)

No longer, Butz believed, would the government need to artificially shore up farm prices by shorting the market of its annual supply of grain, either by imposing restrictions on the amount of grain farmers could plant and market or by promising to buy up any surplus. No longer would farmers have to check with Uncle Sam before making their springtime planting decisions. They would be free to grow for the market and

Figure 3-1 U.S. Exports of Wheat and Feed Grains

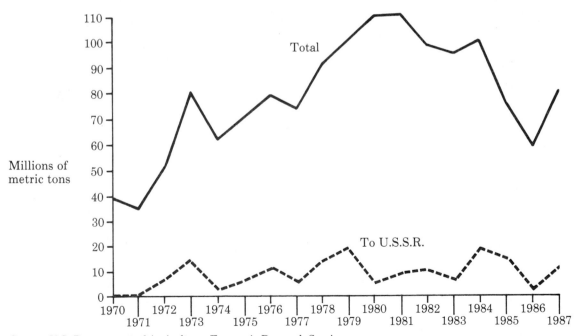

Source: U.S. Department of Agriculture, Economic Research Service.

prosper at it.

In the 1950s and 1960s, U.S. farmers had produced for the relatively static needs of American consumers, who purchased about the same amount of food and fiber every year and paid only slight regard to the price. As such, farm production was not a pure supply-demand industry. It was affected more by technological leaps in production techniques and changes in the weather than by the buying habits of consumers.

With food demand constant, and farm production mainly at the mercy of the elements, farmers looked to the government to control the year-to-year fluctuations in prices and supply.

The 1972 grain deal with the Soviets changed a large part of that relationship. Suddenly, farmers had a new, seemingly limitless market for their bountiful cash crops of wheat and feed grains. The Soviets not only bought up that year's production, they also quickly cleaned out U.S. grain bins of surplus stocks that had been building up for a decade.

In addition, a new international capital market emerged to finance trade. The lack of competition from foreign countries and the growth in purchasing power around most of the world—thanks in large part to the increasing value of their currencies in relation to the dollar—combined to boost demand dramatically for U.S. farm products. The "natural" forces of supply and demand worked both to expand world trade and to increase the U.S. share in trade at an unheard-of rate.

Foreign food consumption grew by 34 million tons a year, far outpacing the 24 million tons a year increase that non-U.S. grain producers could manage. U.S. farmers stepped in to fill the void. After harvesting a total of 293 million acres in 1970, about the same as they had grown annually for the previous decade, farmers boosted their harvested acreage over the next ten years to 352 million acres. Annual grain production climbed from 200 million tons to as high as 300 million.

El Niño Returns

The 1972 grain deal started the new era. Then came El Niño, which sealed its fate.

As usual, El Niño developed in the Pacific just before Christmas and moved south along the coast of Peru. As before, its warm waters wiped out the plentiful anchovy and other delicate marine species that cannot tolerate changes in temperature. It was a momentous occurrence, because anchovy meal is used worldwide as a protein-rich feed supplement for poultry and livestock, and Peruvian fishers supplied about 80 percent of the total demand. Before 1972 the Peruvian government had been able to plan for these temporary droughts in anchovy catches by stocking surpluses. But in the winter of 1972-1973, El Niño's pattern changed. It stayed longer than usual. Anchovies did not return for months.

This freak ecological occurrence set the stage for a series of U.S. actions that, coming on the heels of the Russian grain deal, solidified the now mutually dependent relationship between farmer and government. When Peru could not fulfill its existing fish-meal contracts that season, world agriculture markets went into a frenzy. Animal feeders, desperate to come up with a suitable protein replacement, immediately looked to the United States' massive stocks of feed grains. But these were already committed to the Soviet Union.

So buyers quickly began to elbow each other out for contracts in the only protein-rich commodity left—soybeans. Once a minor cog in the U.S. food-production factory, soybean growers only recently had found an expanding market for their product, mainly soybean oil products sold to Japan. When the anchovy meal supply dried up, however, soybeans became the most desirable feed supplement around. Within weeks, speculators bid up the price on soybeans from $3.00 a bushel to as much as $12.90.

It was the best thing that had ever happened to U.S. farmers. And it had to be stopped.

The Nixon administration, as it happened, had been trying to control inflation and went so far as to impose wage and price controls on U.S. industry in the effort. The runaway price of soybeans, however, threatened to trigger the automatic release of those controls on other food prices and farm wages. Higher soybean prices also threatened to drive up the price of beef and disrupt domestic livestock production. And beyond that, there was a growing concern that the United States might experience its own food shortage by exporting too much of its grain.

President Richard Nixon and his secretary of agriculture, Earl Butz, pictured above, wrapped up a historic grain purchase agreement with the Soviet Union in the summer of 1972.

Over the next few months Nixon and Butz were under intense political pressure to step in. So in June 1973, Nixon took the drastic step of putting a federal embargo on all exports of soybeans and other high-protein feedstuffs. The objective was simple: Allow farmers to sell only to U.S. customers, and grain dealers would be stuck with more soybeans on hand than they could sell. The oversupply would force soybean prices down.

The embargo lasted only a couple of months, but its effects lingered for years and could still be felt in the late 1980s. Japan's response was crucial, since the Japanese were already sensitive about their import vulnerability and what seemed at the time to be a world shortage in foodstuffs.

After the soybean shock, the Japanese began to voice doubts about the reliability of U.S. exports, and they started to invest heavily in Brazilian soybean farms. In 1978, the Japanese government proposed a joint farming venture in Brazil's vast (and previously untouched) Cerrado region, in the stated interest of increasing the world's food supply. By 1987 the original $50 million project had grown to a $300 million enterprise, with a goal of producing 100 million tons annually by the year 2000.

Several countries, including Canada, Australia, and others in Europe and South America, have since geared up their grain production capacity by developing various subsidies and production incentives. The United States remained the largest farm exporting country in the world through the 1970s, but from that time onward U.S. farmers were forced to do business in the highly volatile arena of world politics and competitive world of export markets.

The Tinkering Continues

The U.S. government, of course, has remained a partner in the enterprise.

The 1973 soybean embargo was followed by limited moratoriums on grain exports in 1974 and 1975, which were attempts to deal with the uncertainty of grain supplies and purchases by the Soviet Union. Then in 1980, following the Soviet invasion of Afghanistan, President Jimmy Carter played his agricultural trump card against Moscow. Carter placed a near-total grain embargo on exports to the Soviet Union, one that lasted for sixteen months. To compensate U.S. farmers for their losses from the embargo, the Carter administration was forced to offer a big increase in price-support rates for wheat and corn. With the blessing of Congress, other farm program benefits were also sweetened.

President Reagan rescinded the Soviet embargo shortly after he took office in January 1981, in fulfillment, he said, of

his campaign promise to get the government off the backs of farmers. But in the farm policy debate that followed that year, the administration found no favor in Congress for its plan to phase out farm income supports and drop a number of production-control programs.

Since then Reagan has not been averse to using agriculture as a tool of his foreign policy and political strategies. He consistently has resisted calls from lawmakers to include the Soviet Union in an export-subsidy program. Yet in the weeks preceding the 1986 elections, the president relented and made a token subsidy offer to the Soviets, mainly to placate nervous farm-state Republican senators up for reelection. It did not work. The administration did not come down far enough in its offer to get even a nibble from the Soviets. And the Republicans lost control of the Senate. The next year the administration swallowed its ideological pride and gave the Soviets an offer they could not refuse. The result: the government had to subsidize the sale of 4 million metric tons of wheat with taxpayer funds. Ironically, the Reagan offer to the Soviet Union allowed the "Evil Empire," as he once called it, to acquire grain at prices substantially below those paid by food manufacturers in the United States.

When the anchovy meal supply dried up in 1973 because of El Niño, soybeans became the most desirable feed supplement and their price skyrocketed.

The Reagan administration also supervised the largest "supply management" program in history—the 1983 PIK program that gave government-owned grain to farmers who agreed not to plant their crops. And extending that supply-management policy one step further, the government in 1985 began paying farmers to take up to 45 million acres of land out of production for at least ten years. One purpose of this "conservation reserve" is to protect the most fragile and erodible acres of farm land. A second and more politically compelling reason for the program is to scale back the U.S. agricultural production base, which had put so much cropland into use that U.S. farmers overwhelmed an already glutted grain market. In effect the government tried to maintain high prices by cutting production and limiting supply, a policy that was undercut by stepped-up production in other countries.

"We've played the role of the Saudis in OPEC—we are a one-sided restriction on supply, while everyone else keeps expanding and planting and counting on us to keep the price up," said David Hull, an Agriculture Department economist.

In 1986, the administration, in response to Congress's directive, began issuing the first wave of what would amount to more than $8 billion worth of newly minted payment-in-kind certificates, which are paid to farmers in lieu of cash subsidies. Pete V. Domenici, R-N.M., former chairman of the Senate Budget Committee, has called it "new currency." It has become one of the most popular government programs ever introduced in farm country. A principal feature of the program, from policy makers' point of view, is the government's ability to manipulate market prices by controlling the amount of certificates released and by setting the price at which they can be redeemed for grain. The larger the number of certificates put in circulation, and the lower the redemption price, the more the government affects market behavior. The program caused corn prices, in particular, to drop far below the government's nominal "price floor," the traditional price-support rate as established in farm law.

The Big Fall

Despite most government efforts to maintain equilibrium in the farm economy, the forces that had spurred the agricultural prosperity of the 1970s suddenly turned around in the early 1980s. The increases in world demand fell from 34 million tons of grain a year to 19 million. Foreign grain production, meanwhile, began increasing by 29 million tons a year. Consequently, the 10-million-ton-per-year net increase in grain imported by foreign nations during the 1970s was replaced by a 10-million-ton annual decline during the 1980s.

In 1987, self-sufficiency in wheat production again took its toll on the wheat markets. Although world wheat consumption climbed to a record 507 million tons that year, the quantity imported by wheat-consuming nations was only 85 million tons, or only 17 percent of the total, one of the lowest percentage levels of imports on record.

Policy analysts and politicians argue over what precipitated the fall—whether it was the macroeconomic policies of the newly elected Reagan administration, which dampened demand for U.S. farm products by raising the value of the dollar (and thus the price of grain) relative to other currencies; or the miscalculated price-support policies embedded in the major farm programs reauthorization bill of 1981, which served to stimulate supply. Predictably, the administration and the farm-state coalition in Congress tend to blame each other.

According to the view held by Democrats (and many farm-state Republicans), Reagan's desire to cut taxes led to a mix of U.S. fiscal and monetary policies that all but destroyed U.S. export sales. The combination of rising budget deficits and a tight money supply (enforced by the independent Federal Reserve Board) forced inflation-adjusted interest rates to postwar highs. The rise in the value of the dollar made U.S. products more expensive than competing nations' products, and a worldwide recession reduced demand for U.S. exports.

The U.S. share of world farm exports, after rising from 14.3 percent in 1970 to 19.3 percent in 1981, declined to 14.8 percent in 1987. U.S. feed grain exports alone dropped from 72 percent of the world market to 38 percent from 1981 to 1987.

"Largely, the overall macroeconomic policies we've followed over the past few years have caused our agriculture trade to drop precipitously," said Charles Riemenschnieder, staff director of the Senate Agriculture Committee. "You can't ignore the value of the dollar in that whole equation. And a tight monetary-loose fiscal policy—whether that's good domestic policy is another question; but agriculture has borne a disproportionate share of that burden. The center of the country has not benefited."

On the other hand, say administration officials, the misguided policies in the 1981 farm bill caused irreparable damage to the farm economy. Unnecessarily high price supports, implemented in the expectation of continued high inflation, made it more profitable for U.S. farmers to forfeit their output to the government than to sell it at lower world prices. And because government benefits were contingent upon how much a farmer could produce, administration officials contend, farmers kept expanding their production base. The United States saw record crop production in 1981, 1982, and 1985, even as demand for U.S. farm products steadily dwindled.

Government support prices also indirectly underwrote the expansion of foreign grain production. With U.S. prices high, foreign grain producers could afford the expensive start-up costs associated with building an agriculture infrastructure and still market their products below the U.S. government's price floors. "We are the inadvertent guarantor—we underwrite production throughout the world," said Randall Davis, former associate director in charge of natural resource policy for the Office of Management and Budget. As a result of the price-support policies of the 1981 farm bill, Davis maintained, "we're seeing a number of countries that were never agricultural producers or exporters get into the export business."

Endogenous Zone

When agriculture was booming during the 1970s, farm price-support programs were relatively inexpensive. But with the farm economy mired in a depression, and major grain and cotton producers getting less money for their products, the taxpayer is making up the difference in price- and income-support payments to farmers. "The agriculture budget is endogenous—it is determined by the markets," explained Rausser of the Council of Economic Advisers (CEA).

Rausser was the chief author of a special chapter on agriculture in the CEA's annual report on the economy to the president and Congress in 1987. He argued in that report and in interviews that federal farm programs have distorted the workings of the agricultural economy. "Public policies have been designed to reduce the risk associated with ... commodity prices," he wrote. "When the government guarantees farmers a certain price, for instance, it absorbs risk and eliminates some of

58

the uncertainty."

Yet that is only one side of the farmer-government equation. What has solidified the relationship is the way domestic and trade policies of importing and exporting countries have insinuated themselves into the world agriculture economy. What Congress and the administration now do with U.S. agriculture policy largely determines what happens to commodity prices all over the world.

Each variation in U.S. trade relations or in farm price-support programs, altered one way or another to solve one problem or another, can send tremors through commodity markets that are felt for days, months, years at a time. Many times just a rumor of impending government action will send speculators into a trading frenzy.

"Government itself has also created risks by contributing to commodity market instability," Rausser said. "The [1977] farm bill changed commodity programs to permit a wider fluctuation in prices. The export embargo of 1980 . . . the payment-in-kind program of 1983, and the issuance of generic certificates of 1986, to name but a few large government agricultural programs, make it clear that policy uncertainty can be a major contributor to private commodity market instability."

The Social Contract

On the face of it, federal farm policy does appear to be working at cross-purposes. It is designed ostensibly to stabilize farm prices to the benefit of farmer, consumer, and taxpayer. Yet the government's attempts to intervene are a large factor in agriculture's unstable economic climate. The paradox is not lost on farm policy makers.

"What we've got now is social planning, pure and simple," said Randall Davis. "But it's bad social planning because it's based on 1930s' concepts of how to go about it. It's as if we'd made a decision to save the concept of the corner grocery store. Why, as a matter of social policy, should we be guaranteeing the same number of corner grocery stores? Is that the kind of thing the government should be involved in?"

But then, farm-state lawmakers ask, can U.S. farmers be expected to operate profitably against other nation's producers who are subsidized heavily by their governments?

"How else are you going to compete?" argued Edward R.

Like many otherwise conservative Republicans, Edward R. Madigan of Illinois questioned how U.S. farmers could compete without government support against other countries' producers who are heavily subsidized.

Madigan, a Republican from Illinois and ranking minority member of the House Agriculture Committee. "If we're going to keep an agriculture plant in the United States, then we're going to have to have the government supporting that plant in order to compete," he said. "You either get every [country] to quit doing that, or you have to stay in the game, too."

Economist Martin Abel takes another, more pragmatic view of the farm question. "Once one accepts the proposition that there are legitimate roles for government to play in agriculture, only the degree of involvement is subject to debate," he said. In *Choices,* a journal published by the American Agricultural Economics Association, and in a subsequent interview, Abel maintained that the age-old relationship between government and agriculture is an inescapable product of farming's unique place in developed economies.

"In most countries of the world, agriculture is viewed as a public utility, to be regulated in the interest of society," Abel said. "It is but a small step, politically—although possibly a costly one—from providing a safety net against extremely low prices to protecting farm income.

"Economists have been frustrated for a long time by the fact that agricultural policies distort market prices," he continued. "But such distortions are ubiquitous. Economic efficiency does not carry much weight in the minds of policy makers. Some attention is paid to the cost of agricultural policies in extreme situations, but the notion that governments have a legitimate right to intervene is rarely challenged by society as a whole."

For that reason, agriculture policy has become a political, as well as economic, tool for successive presidents and Congresses. As the actual number of U.S. farmers has dwindled, they have, if anything, only intensified their social and political importance in American life. Farm states play critical roles for both parties in presidential races and in the balance of power in the Senate. The inexorable demographic changes in rural society, though long under way, are reason for members of both parties to support government intervention in agriculture—if only to show they care about an embattled class of taxpaying citizens.

Thus, politicians regularly pay homage to the concept of the family farmer as a national ideal worthy of preservation. Republican and Democrat alike hold up the family farmer as the paragon of the nation's cultural identity.

"It's clear that our farm policies are failing to achieve the basic goal of preserving opportunity for a good life in rural America," Richard Gephardt once said, while another farm-state lawmaker, Rep. Byron L. Dorgan, Democrat of North Dakota, chimed in: "Farm policy should be geared toward the philosophy that we intend to maintain a network of family farmers in this country."

Senate minority leader Robert Dole, Republican of Kansas and a powerful defender of farm interests, who unsuccessfully sought the Republican nomination for president in 1988, suggested that this image of a proud farmer working the land to feed a nation is a moving force in Congress. "There's a lot of empathy about the American farmer, whether it's in Iowa or Kansas or Texas or New Hampshire or Massachusetts," he said. "So I believe there's an understanding on the part of the consuming public that, notwithstanding the cost, they still have a pretty good food bargain.

"I would guess when I first came to Congress [in 1961], maybe a majority thought the government ought to get out of agriculture," Dole added. "Maybe that's still the majority. But I'm not certain."

Chapter 4

Farm Coalition

From Wisconsin to Texas to North Carolina—from milk to cotton to tobacco and corn—the politics of federal agriculture programs have always been defined by the so-called farm coalition, a jovial—if sometimes cantankerous—confederation of rural-oriented lawmakers and farm lobby organizations. The members of this eclectic group, despite their oft-competing interests, long ago discovered that peanut growers in Georgia, say, would be best served in Congress if they supported bean farmers in Michigan. And vice versa.

This friendly working relationship stood farmers well for half a century—so well, in fact, that for most of that time farmers were divided more by general political ideology than by specific region or crop. Their main representatives in Washington were large, general-interest farm organizations whose members included all types of farmers. Many of these groups began not as Washington lobbyists but as service organizations selling insurance and other goods and services to farmers. They formed the nucleus of the farm-state network that sought basic economic protections from the government and found willing listeners in a Congress dominated by like-minded rural representatives.

The largest and best known of the old-line super groups is the American Farm Bureau Federation, which claims nearly two million farm families as members. It has been the mouthpiece for the more prosperous farmers of the Midwestern Corn Belt and the South. Although the Farm Bureau supported the original farm policies of the New Deal era, by the late 1980s the national organization was known mainly for its general disdain for federal farm programs and support for President Reagan's conservative brand of politics. Yet, as its name implies, the bureau is really a "federation" of independent state farm bureaus, which often go their own ways politically when it suits their local members to do so. For example, southeastern branches back the government's strict allotment and quota program for tobacco, while the Wisconsin Farm Bureau parts company with the national organization on dairy policy.

Another mainstay in the farm lobby pantheon is the National Farmers Union (NFU), which claims nearly a million farm families as members and was one of the first advocates of the "family farmer"—one who owns a farm and operates it chiefly with family labor. The NFU had its greatest strength in Oklahoma, Montana, Colorado, Utah, Wisconsin, Minnesota, the Dakotas, and Nebraska, and in general has taken a liberal stance on the issues in opposition to the Farm Bureau. The NFU favored high price supports, saying that the end of the price-support system would mean the end of the family farmer and ultimately the capture of U.S. agriculture by commercial and processing interests.

The National Grange, although less liberal in its approach to farm policy than the NFU, has also favored high price supports. It is one of the supporters of the "marketing loan" system of price supports, which allows farmers to sell their grain at whatever the market brings with a guarantee that the government will make up the difference between the market price and a predetermined support price. Another group, the National Farmers Organization, is typical of the service-oriented nature of the general interest groups. It began and has continued as a bargaining agent for farmers, enabling them to contract directly with commodity buyers. Its politics are more closely aligned with the NFU than the Farm Bureau.

The American Agricultural Movement (AAM) was born out of the "tractorcade" invasions of Washington and other cities in 1978-1979, when discontented farmers protested against President Jimmy Carter's farm policy. The AAM complained then that government was not protecting the interests of all farmers, and the organization has survived to become the most vocal, if not the chief, representative of the sometimes angry faction of farmers who believe Washington still has not done enough for the "little guys" among them. While the AAM has maintained its activist approach to farm lobbying—bringing scores of farm-

ers wearing "AAM" caps to Washington to sit in on Agriculture Committee deliberations—it has also evolved into a politically savvy organization not afraid to get involved in the nuts and bolts of policy making.

The American Agricultural Movement maintains an activist approach to farm lobbying, bringing scores of farmers to Washington to be heard.

Commodity Groups and Special Interests

Yet, while farm organizations remain strong forces in U.S. farm policy, if only because of their size and long histories as voices for farmers, the bloated size of the agriculture budget and the pressures on each interest group to protect its own programs have changed the way farm lobbies work. The traditional fixtures have given way to a newer and smaller type of Washington advocate. The dominant farm group specializes in single commodities or else is a hybrid representing both growers and processors. The individual commodity organizations—soybeans, cotton, pork, cattle, and even honey and sunflowers—will often go different ways to meet the demands of their constituencies.

When this happens, conflict follows quickly. Any favor Congress does for one group invariably has negative repercussions on another. Corn farmers fighting for high grain prices will be opposed quickly by dairy farmers who must buy corn to feed their cows. But then dairy farmers, who may favor slaughtering cowherds to cut back production and boost prices, will run counter to cattle ranchers, who fear the dumping of dairy cows onto the beef market, driving down their own profits.

Toss into this mix consumers, conservation groups, fertilizer and pesticide manufacturers, agribusiness, and the banking and investment community—in other words, a gamut of interest groups affected by government agricultural policies—and the potential conflicts become obvious. Congress, as a result, must then placate several interests at once, or none at all.

Farmers protested against President Jimmy Carter's farm policy with "tractorcade" invasions of Washington, D.C., and other cities in 1978-1979.

Patchwork Farm Legislation

The 1985 farm bill was the paragon example of how farm-state members of Congress managed to bridle all the competing interests to fashion broad, patchwork-quilt farm legislation. The results may have pleased few in Congress or the Reagan administration, but, more important politically, they angered fewer.

Partisan politics were the overarching theme of the farm policy debate in 1985, but budget reduction also was a pervasive issue throughout the year, particularly for the key commodity groups that were forced to grapple for dwindling federal benefits. Both House and Senate Agriculture committees spent months trying to whittle the programs to a size that would take care of the special commodity interests of each member and still cut costs enough to ward off a congressional revolt against farm programs by urban members.

The Reagan administration, for its part, had forged an unusual alliance with consumer groups in another concentrated effort to reduce the government's involvement in sugar, dairy, honey, and peanut production.

Often allying itself with urban Democrats, the administration began its assault in the House by firing several broadsides at these treasured farm benefits. But the Democratic leadership made the package put together by the House Agriculture Committee a leadership issue, arguing that every piece of the farm mosaic must remain intact to put added pressure on Reagan and the Republican party. Democratic leaders, including House Speaker Thomas P. O'Neill, Jr., of Massachusetts and Majority Whip Thomas S. Foley of Washington, predicted early on that any amendment to change the substance of the bill would face an uphill fight. It was a promise that was proved on the first roll call—a vote to reduce sugar price supports.

The government supported the price of sugar by paying eighteen cents a pound to refiners who agreed to pass on the benefits to U.S. growers. The government also placed strict quotas on imported sugar to protect against foreign exporters who, according to U.S. sugar producers, dumped surplus sugar on the world market at heavily subsidized prices, often as low as six cents a pound. Thomas J. Downey, a liberal Democrat from New York, and Bill Gradison, an Ohio Republican, proposed to reduce the sugar price support by one cent a pound per year until it reached fifteen cents a pound for the 1988 crop. They also wanted to eliminate a "transportation" factor in the existing law that added about two and one-half cents a pound to the support price. Downey said the sugar program had pushed the domestic price of sugar past what it was in nearly all other nations. And Gradison argued that reducing the support price would open U.S. markets to Caribbean sugar-producing nations that needed money to repay debts to U.S. banks.

But House Agriculture Committee members successfully changed the course of the debate. They insisted that sugar price supports were ensuring a steady price to sugar manufacturers, and, in the process, protecting U.S. jobs. "This will be the first vote on whether we protect American producers and manufacturers this year," said committee chairman E. "Kika" de la Garza, a Democrat who represents Texas sugar growers, in an impassioned floor speech. "This may well be the beginning of a war, if we are going to have a trade war. You cannot desert this industry at it worst hour. We have to fly the flag."

The House decisively rejected the Downey-Gradison sugar amendment, 142-263.

Dairy Lobby Prevails

An even bigger winner may have been the dairy lobby. Tony Coelho, D-Calif., chairman of the Dairy Subcommittee, had been widely criticized for the way he pushed an industry-written dairy bill through the committee. Coelho was known more for his political than legislative skills—as chairman of the House Democratic Congressional Campaign Committee from 1981 until 1987, he controlled the purse strings for the committee's election contributions. He wanted to maintain the campaign fund pipeline between the dairy industry and Democratic party candidates.

But as Dairy Subcommittee chairman, Coelho managed to push the bill through vociferous attacks of Republicans and fellow Democrats alike. The most controversial section of the bill was the revival of a "diversion" program that would pay dairy farmers not to produce milk. (A similar program was in effect for fifteen months during 1984-1985.) The House bill would have continued the diversion program as a way to reduce the massive surpluses of dairy products that the government had been required to buy up through the price-support pro-

Before he became House majority whip in 1987, Tony Coelho, D-Calif., was chairman of the Agriculture Subcommittee on Livestock, Dairy and Poultry while Congress considered the 1985 farm bill.

gram. The bill also would permit the agriculture secretary to buy out whole herds of dairy cows and send them to slaughter as a means to reduce production of milk. Farmers would pay the cost of the diversion and buyout programs themselves, through small assessments on the milk products they sold at market.

As a concession to the livestock industry, which feared a market glut of beef as a result of the dairy herd buyouts, the Agriculture Committee originally included a provision to require the government to buy up $200 million worth of red meat. The House later increased that figure to $250 million in a compromise between Coelho and Doug Bereuter, a Nebraska Republican.

Coelho, who had put together a coalition of competing, regional dairy interests for his "unity" bill, effectively sealed the victory when the House ratified his provision to add geographical "differentials" to the price of milk in regions of the country. Midwestern farmers opposed the differentials because they effectively prevented the sale of surplus Midwestern milk in Southeastern states, where milk sold at high, deficit-induced prices. But representatives from pivotal New England districts refused to go along with Midwestern efforts to strip the differentials from the bill. That gave Coelho a solid front among various regional interests, including Republicans from the Midwest and New England, enabling him hold off an assault on the rest of the bill by the administration and consumer groups.

Not even the acid tongue of Barney Frank, a Massachusetts Democrat who rarely missed an opportunity to poke fun at farm programs, could penetrate Coelho's armor. Arguing that dairy subsidies had only encouraged farmers to produce more than the market would bear, Frank remarked: "We now have enough butter to slather Wyoming into complete slipperiness."

Nevertheless, an amendment by James R. Olin, Democrat from Virginia, and Robert H. Michel, an Illinois Republican and House minority leader, to make annual reductions in dairy price supports and eliminate the diversion program failed on a 166-244 vote.

Reagan Administration Lost Ground

Republican leaders later conceded that the Reagan administration, as a result of the defeats on dairy and sugar, lost considerable ground in its efforts to scale back price- and income-support benefits in the remaining sections of the bill. In the end, the farm coalition held fast and won all but one key vote: an alternative plan to let farmers themselves vote on strict production controls for their crops. As it turned out, that was the one issue on which the House leadership itself was divided.

Foley, who opposed all forms of mandatory controls, had grudgingly allowed the referendum amendment to be attached to the committee's bill in an effort to win the votes of key Democrats, who had threatened to mutiny unless such a provision was included. But House Republicans mobilized a campaign to defeat it while Foley and de la Garza, who had been insisting that the entire committee bill remain intact, offered only mild defense. The mandatory controls amendment was summarily defeated on the floor, 174-251, before the bill was approved 282-141.

Though hardly mentioned in the 1985 farm bill debate, one of the largest sections of the bill was devoted to continuing and expanding the government's food nutrition programs, including food stamps, which had been one of the government's main antipoverty tools since President Lyndon B. Johnson's Great Society campaign of the 1960s.

The nutrition programs are run by the Agriculture Department, which looks upon them more as an outlet for surplus commodity production than as a service to the poor and elderly. These programs also serve a political purpose, however: since most food stamp benefits go to large urban centers, where the poor are concentrated, that section of the farm bill attracts votes of the growing number of urban lawmakers who might otherwise oppose such expensive support programs for a relatively few (and comparatively well-to-do) number of farmers.

Senate Power Struggle

In the Senate, where farm states hold a considerable balance of power, the political dynamics of the 1985 farm bill were similarly baroque. The Senate Agriculture Committee, under the effective control of minority Democrats and renegade Republicans, wanted a farm bill that sought to protect direct income subsidies to farmers even while it allowed the prices of major crops to fall. But faced with Republican opposition by Chairman Jesse Helms of North Carolina and committee member Robert Dole of Kansas, who was also the Senate majority

The government's food nutrition programs, including food stamps, are run by the Agriculture Department. The programs serve a political purpose in attracting urban lawmakers to support farm legislation.

leader, the bill was bottled up for months. It was sent to the floor only after a deal involving the Agriculture and Finance committees was forged between wheat-state and tobacco-state senators.

Helms and Dole had been unable to fashion a compromise capable of winning bipartisan support. Then Helms, the leading voice in Congress for tobacco interests, came up with a scheme that included tobacco price supports, one of the few farm programs in real jeopardy of being eliminated by Congress.

Helms had worked out a tenuous deal between cigarette manufacturers and tobacco growers to roll back government loan rates and assess the companies as well as growers for all of the subsidy program's cost, which had become so burdensome to growers that they were ready to abandon the program. In return, Helms's deal gave the companies effective control over the government's system of acreage allotments and tobacco quotas, governing how much growers could plant and sell each year.

71

Although several other tobacco-state legislators were included in the discussions that led to the controversial agreement, its path through Congress was not ensured. Helms's North Carolina rival, Democratic representative Charlie Rose, who claimed to be working on the growers' behalf in opposition to the manufacturers, had put together a different plan in the House. His plan would use two cents of the existing sixteen-cent excise tax on cigarettes to pay for the tobacco price-support program. Tobacco companies, for their part, were vigorously opposed to the high excise tax, which was coming up for renewal that year.

Recognizing the hostile environment in the House as well as in his own Agriculture Committee, Helms looked for another way to get his tobacco plan adopted. He eventually cut a deal with Dole, who was also a member of the Senate Finance Committee, to attach the price-support plan to a Finance bill making the expiring excise tax permanent. The maneuver drew howls of protest from Democrats who said the Finance Committee was in no position to judge the merits of a major agriculture bill. Among those protesting were Democrats David Boren of Oklahoma and David Pryor of Arkansas, Finance Committee members who also sat on Agriculture.

But as often happens in farm coalition politics, the four farm-state politicians found a way to satisfy everyone's basic interests. They reached an agreement that would allow Helms to get his tobacco plan through the Finance Committee and also open the door for the Agriculture Committee to report a farm bill—though, as it turned out, not exactly the bill Helms and Dole wanted.

Once again, the Agriculture Committee's efforts to craft agriculture policy showed that the old farm-coalition mentality could override even intensely partisan loyalties. In a key 10-7 committee vote, two Republican defectors, Mark Andrews of North Dakota and Mitch McConnell of Kentucky, joined the panel's eight Democrats in support of slightly increasing and then freezing direct subsidies for grain farmers for the life of the four-year bill. Andrews, who was up for reelection in 1986, had been a staunch ally of Democrats who favored higher income subsidies. Freshman McConnell, on the other hand, had sat silently through three months of markup action on the farm bill, faithfully voting with Helms and Dole on every provision.

McConnell changed his vote only after Dole struck the deal

Sen. David Boren, D-Okla., pictured above, dealt in some old-fashioned vote trading with Sen. Mitch McConnell, R-Ky., on the 1985 farm bill.

Senators Edward Zorinsky, D-Neb., Jesse Helms, R-N.C., and Robert Dole, R-Kan., are pictured, left to right, holding all thirteen pounds of the 1985 farm bill before the Senate gave its final approval.

with Helms on tobacco, the main agricultural product in McConnell's home state. The ploy took most Agriculture Democrats by surprise. But Boren and Pryor eventually agreed to drop their opposition to Dole's tobacco amendment in return for McConnell's vote for their farm package and Helms's promise to let a Democratic-sponsored farm bill go to the floor.

Afterwards, McConnell and Boren were unapologetic about their blatant vote trading. "My only interest is in the 150,000 people in Kentucky who grow tobacco," McConnell said, adding that his commitment to the Democrats was only temporary. "I have cooperated in getting [the farm bill] out on the floor. I'm not bound by that vote on the floor," he said.

Said Boren: "We're attempting to rebuild the farm coalition."

Farm Bill Horse Trading

Dole eventually took the reins of the farm bill on the floor and, through a combination of parliamentary skill and legislative doublespeak, managed to fashion a bill that contained a little bit of something for nearly everyone.

At the heart of Dole's package were two contradictory methods of dealing with target prices, the benchmark of federal farm income subsidies. The Senate Agriculture Committee, dominated by Democrats and farm-state Republicans, had reported a bill that would have frozen target prices for wheat, feed grains, cotton, and rice at then-current levels for four more years. The administration and other GOP leaders, on the other hand, wanted to begin cutting back on target prices right away.

Like Andrews, several other farm-state Republicans were up for reelection in 1986, and with the GOP holding a slim 53-47 majority in the Senate, Democrats made the farm bill a central plank in their strategy to regain control of the chamber. They focused most of their energy on the four-year target price freeze, to evident early success. When Richard G. Lugar, an Indiana Republican, offered an amendment to begin cutting target prices within a year, twelve Republicans defected from party ranks and voted against the Lugar cuts. Ten of the twelve were from Farm Belt states.

After that vote, Dole placed a parliamentary lock on the Senate until he could come up with a package to placate both the administration, which treatened to veto any bill with a four-year freeze on target prices, and farm-state Republicans, who did not want to be identified with a farm bill that cut income subsidies. He used the privilege of his leadership position in the Senate to keep control of the floor and prevent Democrats from offering their own Republican-baiting amendments.

In the meantime Dole, looking for some middle ground between a four-year freeze and a one-year freeze, found a novel legislative solution: He included both. The result was that each section of the bill dealing with a particular commodity's target prices had two contradictory provisions—a one-year freeze acceptable to the administration and conservative Republicans, and a four-year freeze acceptable to many farm-state Republicans and Democrats. Although the two provisions technically cancelled each other out, Dole said he would leave it to a House-Senate conference to choose between them.

Yet six farm-state Republicans continued to balk and voted against the Dole package. To make up for their defections, Dole resorted to some old-fashioned horse trading among senators who represented various commodity and regional interests. He induced some fiscally conservative Democrats to vote for several cost-saving devices, including one to take more land (used to grow price-supported grain) out of production. He brought over rice-state senators from Arkansas and Mississippi with three new provisions designed to expand benefits for rice producers, including one to cover the 1985 crop that would not otherwise have been part of the new farm bill.

He also won votes of senators representing sugar-cane growers in the Gulf states and Hawaii, and sugar beet growers in the Dakotas and Minnesota, with a plan to protect their domestic markets. The deal came much to the chagrin of Reagan's State and Treasury departments. Dole's sugar provision effectively forced the administration to reduce the flow of imported sugar into the United States, even as State and Treasury were working to increase the flow of sugar from debt-ridden Caribbean nations that needed hard U.S. currency to pay off massive U.S. bank debts.

Dole also increased authority for giving disaster benefits to Gulf-state farmers whose crops had been ruined by hurricanes. He gave corn-state senators a provision that would guarantee farmers a certain income subsidy regardless of how market prices turn. And he included a section written by the American Soybean Association to give farmers a flat payment of $30 an acre and a payment-in-kind (PIK) of $5 an acre worth of government-owned crops.

With the help of those legislative sweeteners, Dole appeared to have enough votes for his farm bill package. The bait-and-switch routine reached its comic zenith when Mark Andrews bounded out of the Senate chamber toward the majority leaders's office and, in the presence of reporters waiting outside, yelled out to a Dole aide: "Wait! I've got one more." So in a final bow to Andrews, who up to that point had been a consistent ally of Democrats on farm policy, Dole added $35-an-acre payments to sunflower producers, most of whom were in North Dakota and who were not eligible for other farm support programs.

In the end, Dole lured eleven Democrats to his package and won over six Republicans (including Andrews) who earlier had voted against a one-year freeze in target prices. While his package contained blatantly contradictory language on target prices, the ultimate impact of his tactics was a defeat for Senate Democrats. The Senate eventually adopted a compromise on the target price issue, which was further modified in a conference with the Democratically controlled House. Some of Dole's sweeteners—notably, the soybean and sunflower provisions— were discarded in the conference. But the sugar and rice provisions for southern producers remained.

Dole, in still another deft maneuver, also made his presence felt in a House-Senate showdown on dairy policy. House Democrats won their biggest victory over the Reagan administration when Senate conferees finally gave in on the new program to reduce milk surpluses by requiring the government to buy up entire herds of dairy cows. Dole held the key vote among the five Republican and four Democratic Senate conferees, and he finally sided with the Democrats. "He became a kingpin," said Coelho. "We didn't reach a deal until Dole walked in the door."

'The Ship's Back In'

The deft footwork of Dole, Coelho, and other experts in farm-state politics was standard procedure in Congress during the 1985 farm bill debate and the subsequent election year of 1986. In each legislative battle the fingerprints of particular commodity groups and other special interests were evident, especially so as the race to control the Senate intensified. Both Democrats and Republicans went out of their way to help farmers in a high-stakes game of partisan gamesmanship, and the commodity groups were their main avenue to rural voters.

Another good example of the farm coalition at work came in 1987—after the election was over and in a time of relative partisan harmony in agriculture.

The Senate Agriculture Committee, now under Democratic control, was conducting its first business meeting of the One-hundredth Congress. The January 1987 session was called to mark up a bill by Oklahoma's Boren. He maintained that a $400 million disaster program, created by Congress in October 1986 in response to widespread drought in the Southeast and heavy flooding throughout the Midwest, inadvertently excluded winter wheat, his state's main crop. Floods kept many farmers from planting their 1987 crops, which had to be seeded in late 1986. Boren said his bill would rectify Congress's original intent to aid

Farmers long ago learned to increase their voices in Washington through organization and political activism. Pictured is a meeting of Western farmers, 1956.

farmers who suffered losses during 1986 as a result of "drought, excessive heat, flood, hail or excessive moisture."

The one-time disaster payment program had been folded into the fiscal 1987 governmentwide appropriations bill over the objections of the administration. It provided PIK certificates, which could be redeemed for government-owned grain, to farmers in federally designated disaster counties. Farmers were eligible to get up to $100,000 each in PIK certificates to cover heavy losses in their expected 1986 harvests. Farmers of the major, federally subsidized crops of wheat, feed grains, cotton, and rice were eligible for benefits, as were farmers of "non-program" specialty crops that were afflicted by "drought, excessive heat, flood, hail, or excessive moisture." Those guidelines covered innumerable cases of hardship resulting from a devastating drought in the Southeast in the summer of 1986 and massive flooding in the Midwest later that autumn.

Spinach growers in Oklahoma, pinto bean farmers in Michigan, and tobacco planters in Tennessee were among farmers in thirty-eight states and U.S. territories who applied in droves for disaster benefits. An Agriculture Department official said that one South Carolina farmer wanted relief to cover losses the drought caused to his daffodils. "It wasn't just a garden plot," the official said. "This guy had 60 acres of daffodils."

A banana grower in Guam applied but was not eligible for benefits, the department ruled, because Guam was not an officially designated disaster area. But vegetable growers in the Pacific islands of Saipan, Tinian, and Ponape were eligible. The crops in those U.S. territories in the North Pacific were wiped out by typhoons, the official said, "which were excessive moisture, you might say."

In fact, more than 200,000 farmers sent in applications for more than $500 million in disaster benefits. The administration had ruled that payments would be prorated to all eligible farmers out of the $400 million appropriated by Congress, meaning recipients would get less than eighty cents for every one dollar of losses they incurred.

Into that hot political climate came Boren and his claim that winter wheat growers in the Midwest were left out of the eligibility list. Agriculture Department officials estimated that three million acres of winter wheat were not planted in 1986 because the soil was flooded. Adding those farmers into the program would cost another $130 million.

But when Boren started looking for support for his bill, he discovered that other senators were hearing from farmer-constituents who believed their own weather horror stories should qualify them for benefits, too. "We had been telling our people, 'Sorry, the ship's already left the port,' " an aide to Jesse Helms said. "So here comes the first bill of the new Congress and—lo and behold—the ship's back in."

To win approval for legislation that would benefit farmers mainly in Oklahoma and neighboring Kansas, Boren had to open up the bill to his colleagues' regional concerns. The resulting dialogue among the committee members during a meeting on his bill spoke volumes about the state of the farm coalition.

Singing 'Jingle Bells'

The first amendment to Boren's bill came from Helms, the former chairman. "Would you tell me why freezing loss is not included? You've got heat," Helms asked. "We've got some apple growers down in North Carolina who are mad as a wet hen because that's excluded, and they had a terrible loss last year."

Helms then looked across the committee's boardroom table to David Pryor, a Democrat from Arkansas: "Got any apple growers?"

"Don't have any apple growers," Pryor replied.

"Peach—you've got peach," interjected Howell Heflin, an Alabama Democrat.

The committee's new chairman, Patrick J. Leahy, then suggested that Helms let the Agriculture Department study the question of paying for apple grove freeze damage and report back to the panel. "Do they have peaches in that [report], too?" Heflin chimed in.

Leahy, already sensing the matter snowballing into what Capitol Hill veterans call a "Christmas tree" bill, played a halfhearted Scrooge. "You don't want me to start singing 'Jingle Bells' up here, do you?" he chided, just before instructing department officials to make their report on "tree crops" in general. "And 'freeze,'" he was reminded. "And 'freeze,' yes. We assume that all crops freeze up where I come from," said the Vermont Democrat, who began making reference to his agricultural roots after a Senate career dominated by other interests.

Sen. Howell Heflin, D-Ala., explained the meaning of a 'moondog' amendment during the course of debate on a disaster-relief bill in 1987.

Next up, Pryor offered a somewhat complicated amendment on cotton. But he had a difficult time explaining how cotton growers deserved special treatment for disaster losses even though their crop yields had not suffered. Price supports for cotton, unlike those for other federally subsidized crops, decrease with the declining quality of the harvested fiber, he tried to say. His proposal would cover those kinds of losses.

Heflin once again leaped to Pryor's rescue. "Really, this amendment, to fully understand it, you have to have plowed behind the south end of a northbound mule," the former Alabama judge began. "This is what you call a 'moondog' amendment," he went on. "There's an old saying . . . that if a farmer looks up in late August, he sees what is called the moondog in the moon. It's a circle around the moon, and if there are spots in the circle that means you are going to have undue moisture at the wrong time.

"They say the moondog will make the bolls turn brown as the eyes of a long-haired dog, you see," Heflin continued. "The old farmers will tell you that your cotton is going to be in terrible condition."

Helms interjected: "Now, he sees all this while he's behind the mule plowing?"

"Well, no," Heflin answered. "It's at night. We don't plow in Alabama at night."

The committee put aside the Pryor-Heflin amendment because it could not agree on its cost, but the sponsors won a commitment to pursue it as part of another bill. Rudy Boschwitz, a Republican from Minnesota who often played devil's advocate in these swap sessions, complained that cotton interests were asking for new benefits from Congress after getting generous treatment in previous farm legislation. "I would point out to my friends from Alabama and Arkansas and Oklahoma that we in Minnesota have some mold in our corn crop," Boschwitz said, adding, "Because of rains . . . there are even more quality problems with respect to soybeans."

"Sauce for the goose, sauce for the gander," observed Lugar, the committee's new ranking Republican. "We better find out every bit of spoilage and moisture we've got and see how many problems we have to cure."

John Melcher, a Montana Democrat, pointed out one more. "We had a fall flood in Montana, which is very unusual," he said. "We've got about 200 ranchers that are involved in [their] hay and straw being destroyed by floods, already baled and sitting in the field."

"I don't understand what occurred," Boschwitz said. "The hay was out in the field and bundled and it got rained on?"

Melcher explained: "Just stacked where it was. The flood took it away."

Boschwitz: "This is not hay that was baled and got rained on, but was swept away by the flood? The Red Sea opened?"

Melcher: "That is correct. This is hay, or straw, that was baled, it was swept away, destroyed by the flood."

Boschwitz: "Swept away—not destroyed, not left there and rendered of less value because it got wet? Gone. Is that right?"

Melcher's hay amendment was adopted, but the panel restricted total payments to $1 million, to be taken out of the $400 million authorized in the original disaster program. No one farmer could get more than $20,000. "How much hay is $20,000 worth?" Lugar wanted to know. "A lot more hay than I raise on my farm in Vermont," Leahy cut in.

Freshman Kent Conrad, D-N.D., new to the committee and to Washington, wondered how his farmer constituents could get such payments. "If we had some extraordinary circumstances in my state, or in South Dakota, obviously they would qualify for this, and be the first guy to the trough?" he asked. "In terms of the million dollars, the first ones to apply for this program. . . ?"

Leahy interrupted him. "Right. Rush to the bank," the chairman said.

The committee then approved Boren's bill, as amended, with a chorus of "ayes." The full Senate passed it with dispatch later that night. As the panel broke up, Heflin mentioned another problem concerning soybeans. But that discussion was postponed for another day.

Chapter 5

Power of the Purse

One day in early 1987, a Michigan member of Congress was describing to his committee chairman, Jamie L. Whitten of Mississippi, the problems of his home-state farmers. Severe flooding in the fall of 1986 had wiped out many of their beet, dry beans, and potato crops. Some would be forced out of business. It was unlikely that a $400 million disaster-relief program, which Congress had just approved that year to take care of weather-related crop failures all over the country, would be large enough to go around. "I told him how my farmers were suffering," recalled Democrat Bob Traxler, who represented the state's rural Thumb district, "and how it seemed like there was nothing we could do for them."

Whitten, the dean of all House members, listened to this sad story, then told his protégé not to worry. "Bob, I've been here a long time," Whitten consoled him, "and I've never seen a disaster that wasn't an opportunity."

Welcome to the *other* world of farm-state politics, the one ruled by Whitten, venerable Democratic chairman of the House Appropriations Committee.

Approaching the age of eighty and nearing his fiftieth year in Congress in the late 1980s, Whitten was the reigning master of political opportunism, especially when it came to money for agriculture. Since 1978 he served as chairman of Appropriations, the spending arm of the House and one of the two most powerful committees (along with tax-writing Ways and Means) in that chamber. But Whitten's real power base always had been the Appropriations Subcommittee on Agriculture, where he had been a dominating chairman since 1949.

Unlike the better known Agriculture Committee, which sets farm policy and writes legislation authorizing the Agriculture Department to carry out those policies, the Appropriations Subcommittee on Agriculture has a different and much less understood function in the House. Its members do not write farm law, as such, but they are no less powerful than their counterparts on the policy-setting, or "authorizing," Agriculture Committee. Whitten's Agriculture panel has unchallenged control over the Agriculture Department's purse strings. It not only holds the checkbook but also writes the checks, deciding each year how much money can be spent for the various agriculture and nutrition programs that come under the department's wide-ranging jurisdiction. With that control over spending emanates as much congressional power and influence as any single farm-state politician could hope for.

The main instrument of Whitten's power is his intimate knowledge of a particular agency of the federal government, one that has no building to identify it and not an employee to its name—though it is, in fact, the ninth-largest corporation in the United States. In Washington and throughout farm country, this phantom institution is known simply as the "CCC," short for Commodity Credit Corporation.

Despite, or possibly because of, its mysterious existence, the CCC has been a pillar of the federal government's farm policy for more than fifty years. Its status has been earned despite the fact that it is only a paper holding company, an accountant's repository for nearly $30 billion worth of crop loans and surplus farm goods. Yet it maintains a palpable grip on the nation's agricultural economy, on Congress, and on the entire federal spending process. Its claim on the Treasury is as close to absolute as generations of farm law have been able to make it. Its unique structure not only gives a stable prop to the farm economy but also gives farm state legislators a tool to garner power far above their numbers in Congress.

What is this strange corporate entity, which borrows money to make loans to farmers who do not have to pay them back? Why does the government continue to use an institution that serves no ostensible purpose, other than to shuffle money from government to farmer, holding Congress and the taxpayers hostage in the process? And how has this arcane system managed to survive for half a century, even avoiding the budgetary swath cut by Gramm-Rudman-Hollings?

Jamie L. Whitten, D-Miss., chairman of the Appropriations Subcommittee on Agriculture since 1949, has had unchallenged control over the Agriculture Department's purse strings.

The answers to these questions go a long way in showing how farm-state members of Congress have managed to wield power and influence in affairs that go beyond the everyday reach of agriculture policy. They show how the convoluted agriculture appropriations process has both everything—and nothing—to do with the exploding costs of farm price-support programs. And they give a good clue to why Whitten is only half-jokingly referred to as the "permanent secretary of agriculture."

The Appropriations Chairman

Whitten and his subcommittee have primary jurisdiction over the CCC, and over the years Whitten has learned better than anyone how to use the CCC's peculiar structure to his political advantage. He employs his seniority status in the House and esoteric knowledge of congressional appropriations as leverage with other power centers in Congress, including the authorizing Agriculture Committee, as well as with the executive branch. The main weapon in his arsenal is the CCC.

On agriculture spending issues, few dare stand in his way. Lynn Martin, of Illinois, vice chairman of the House Republican Conference, remembered one day in 1986 when she took the floor to challenge Whitten on a bill he was trying to bring to the floor. When she sat down afterwards, witnesses said she was visibly shaking. "People kept coming up to me saying they were amazed that I did it," Martin said. "What's worse, I think I won."

Though she succeeded in temporarily blocking Whitten's plans, Martin laughed off the notion that she was marked for his vengeance. "I don't think of him as a vindictive individual. But someone with the shrewdness that Jamie has, and the experience, certainly could find a way to get back at you." She recalled one instance when the House was ready to pass a bill that Whitten had strenuously opposed. Knowing he was going to lose, Whitten forced the bill's sponsors to use a rare voting procedure that required each member to walk down to the well of the chamber and past a teller, who would count the votes. Whitten, of course, used his seniority to get himself appointed to the job of teller. "Nothing was said out loud," Martin said, "but it was obvious as you walked by him that Jamie was taking note of whether you were, or were not, on his side."

Yet for all his time and influence in Congress, the one-time grammar school teacher and county prosecutor from Charleston, Miss., is hardly known beyond Capitol Hill and his home-state political community. He has a reputation for backroom dealing and logrolling on the gritty fiscal issues that concern the Appropriations Committee. At one time his Agriculture post was a virtual fiefdom. But he lost much of his autocratic power after the post-Watergate generation of reform-minded House Democrats stripped his subcommittee of jurisdiction over environmental and consumer issues.

No one, however, questions his central role in federal farm programs. They are the main concern of his local constituency, which remains predominately rural. And though he claimed he personally was not very interested in agriculture when he first came to Congress, Whitten has devoted his career to protecting and expanding the basic structure of farm policy that was created, many years ago, by his generation of legislators.

One of Whitten's shrewdest talents, many colleagues think, is his manner of public speaking. He talks with the dynamic cadence of a Southern planter. But the syntax is often complex and his vocabulary anachronistic. Uncannily, he can speed up his Delta drawl so that words and phrases become incomprehensible. When he is speaking on the floor, veteran reporters have learned to duck down next to the small speakers that carry

Chairman Jamie L. Whitten, standing left, presides over the House Appropriations Committee.

sound to the press gallery in hopes of catching a phrase or two.

Some members think he speaks that way for a reason. "You can always tell how much money is involved by how hard it is to understand him," Martin said. "Whenever I've had a private conversation with Chairman Whitten, I've been able to understand every word he says." She added: "The reason nobody understands the CCC is because nobody understands Jamie Whitten."

Whitten, for his part, merely smiles at the allegation. "People say they can't hear and they can't understand what I say," he said, feigning incomprehension at the charge with a perfectly enunciated reply. "I'm not trying to fool anybody. After all, I'm from north Mississippi. I'm a Yankee member of the delegation."

The CCC and Supplemental Appropriations

Whitten did not create the problem of explosive cost of farm subsidies, which placed the CCC in constant peril in the 1980s. But he did learn to exploit a glaring flaw in the CCC's structure.

Without steady infusions of federal funds, federal price-support programs for farmers stop working, and farmers in every state stop getting the price-support benefits already promised them. No one in Washington wants the blame for that. So nearly every year since 1982, the CCC's unpredictable need for cash made it the subject of "emergency supplemental" appropriations bills. Congress turned these events into an annual excuse for piling on not-so-urgent riders. And the man members had to come to was Whitten. (See Figure 5-1.)

The midyear CCC supplemental bill is the special child of Whitten, who came to Congress in 1941—eight years after the CCC was created. With the CCC under his thumb, Whitten and other farm-state members of the Appropriations Committee possess special leverage in Congress, particularly against conservative Republicans in the White House and in the Senate whose political lifeblood comes straight from farm country.

Unabashedly, Whitten uses the CCC supplemental as an attractive lure for bargains with other members, virtually guaranteeing unquestioned support for whatever his committee wants for agriculture. Ironically, even many of those who criticize the bloated costs of farm programs have become adherents

Figure 5-1 Original and Supplemental Appropriations for the Commodity Credit Corporation

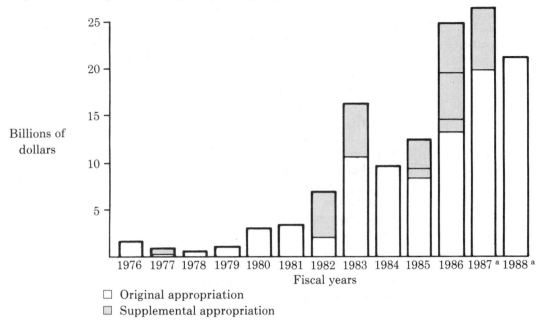

Source: U.S. Department of Agriculture.

Note: Until 1989, the Commodity Credit Corporation (CCC) could borrow up to $25 billion on its own. But appropriations were necessary to reimburse the corporation for net losses incurred when loan repayments did not cover the cost of loans to farmers and for direct expenditures such as income-support payments. Congress increased the CCC's borrowing authorization to $30 billion in 1989.

[a] Requested.

of this peculiar way they are funded. A CCC supplemental can propel social spending past administration veto threats. It can create broad new alliances for projects with otherwise limited appeal. Few other parts of government create such a perennial necessity of legislative life. "More often than not, the CCC has been the engine that's pulled the train," conceded Traxler, employing a congressional cliché that could have been invented for the situation.

As a result, practically every member of Congress has a political stake in keeping the CCC working the way it always has. "It becomes the legislative vehicle for funding every department of government," agreed Thad Cochran, R-Miss., a member of the Senate Appropriations and Agriculture committees and former chairman of the Appropriations Subcommittee on Agriculture. "The CCC [funding bill] is something you know is going to have to come from Congress from time to time, and have to be signed by the president.

"It gives [Whitten] tremendous power," Cochran said. "He knows members of his committee will be needed. They can't be shut out of the process. They end up being very involved in government."

Typically, the supplemental bill has become the vehicle for a range of unrelated spending projects that are important to a majority of members. They know there are not that many opportunities to get controversial legislation through Congress and enacted into law.

The 1987 supplemental appropriations bill reveals the CCC's wide-ranging influence. That measure included $6.7 billion for the CCC, or more than two-thirds of the total $9.4 billion in new, year-end spending authority that Congress approved for the 1987 fiscal year. The other third of the bill included a host of unrelated line-items that, for one reason or another, required more money than they got at the first of the fiscal year. About $1.6 billion went to a new retirement system and a pay increase for federal employees; $137.5 million was for aid to the homeless; $768 million went to the Pentagon; and $300 million was earmarked for aid to Central America.

It is these nonagricultural portions of the supplemental that regularly attract opposition from congressional budget watchers and nonfarm-state members. Senators stalled the bill on budgetary grounds, claiming it would increase the federal deficit by $2.6 billion; then, when it was on the floor, they tried to attach amendments on controversial subjects. During House floor action, members voted to slash the bill by 21 percent, an action that ultimately would not have affected most agriculture programs because Congress simply would have had to come back later with yet another supplemental appropriation for the CCC.

Indeed, the CCC's portion of the bill went through Congress almost without discussion. It is immune from the 1985 Gramm-Rudman-Hollings deficit-reduction law governing spending decisions, and, because of the unique accounting methods used to pay for farm programs, Congress and the Reagan administration had virtually no choice but to approve added funding for the CCC. House leaders tacitly acknowledged the need to use the CCC vehicle to carry other pet spending proposals by refusing to move a "clean" funding bill for CCC alone, even when delays in moving the larger version temporarily shut down farm programs.

Over the years, the CCC supplemental has inspired a number of major nonagricultural policy fights. In 1986, a $5.3 billion supplemental for the CCC became the focus of a confrontation between the administration and Congress over the president's power to refuse to spend previously appropriated money on programs he did not like. In 1985, the supplemental bill was the vehicle for Congress to resume funding for the Nicaraguan contras. Whitten also used it to force settlement of a longstanding dispute over how much state and local governments should contribute to dams and other water projects—with special exemptions for projects in his Mississippi River Valley. A 1983 bill, in addition to $5.7 billion for the CCC, contained a $4.6 billion antirecession jobs package.

Through them all, Whitten served as dealmaker and power broker, virtually by definition: As chairman, he is the originating sponsor of the CCC supplemental. He manages the bill on the House floor, and he cuts the deals when differences crop up between the House's bill and the Senate's. In the end, he usually gets his way.

Thad Cochran, R-Miss., described the Commodity Credit Corporation funding bill as "the legislative vehicle for funding every department of government."

A Flexible Agency for Farmers

The CCC is the source of Whitten's power. For more than fifty years, the Commodity Credit Corporation has been the strong arm of U.S. farm policy. Founded in 1933, it was designed as a fiscal remedy for an unwieldy system, then administered by the Federal Farm Board, of buying up surplus commodities. Farmers continued to produce more each year than they could sell, and the farm board, powerless to control farmers' production decisions, found it impossible to eliminate the annual buildup of surplus stocks. So, in 1933, Congress sought to bolster prices by paying producers to take some of their land out of production.

President Franklin D. Roosevelt in turn created the CCC, signing an executive order to form it as a private corporation chartered in Delaware. This new entity made it possible to put money in farmers' pockets immediately, without waiting for production controls to take effect on market prices. The CCC could make loans to farmers at harvest, so they could afford to hold their products off the market until prices improved.

These nonrecourse loans are still the government's most important tool for stabilizing the prices of the "basic," or storable, commodities—wheat, feed grains, rice, soybeans, and cotton. In return for a short-term loan from the CCC, farmers put up their crops as collateral. If a farmer cannot get a better price at the market than the loan rate from the CCC, all or part of the crop can be forfeited to the corporation; the farmer keeps the principal. The government is left with no other recourse to recoup its loan. In effect, the CCC loan rate becomes a minimum price for the output of participating farmers, making the CCC the buyer of the country's residual supply of those commodities.

In 1948, Congress passed the Commodity Credit Corporation Charter Act (PL 80-806), assigning all rights, duties, assets, and liabilities of the old Delaware corporation to a new, federally chartered entity within the Agriculture Department. Today the CCC is an agency of the government, under the direct supervision of the secretary of agriculture. The CCC's board of directors consists of the secretary and other presidential appointees in the department. It depends on the employees and facilities of the department—mainly the Agricultural Stabilization and Conservation Service, the agency for commodity programs—to carry out its activities in the course of their duties.

Under the wide-ranging terms of its charter, the CCC has become a highly flexible agency that can move in many different directions—acquire stocks of grain and other storable commodities, dispose of stocks, bolster prices, or make payments to farmers—to carry out the various price and income policies of Congress.

The CCC also has practically unbridled authority to sell U.S. commodities on overseas markets, giving it considerable power to affect international trade. In effect, Congress gave the CCC—and thus the executive branch—the authority and financial resources to do whatever it needs to do to support the prices and incomes of farmers.

The CCC can support the prices of commodities through loans, purchases, payments, and other operations. It can procure commodities for sale to other government agencies, foreign governments, and domestic, foreign, or international relief agencies. It can remove and dispose of surpluses. It can try to increase the domestic consumption of farm products by expanding markets. And it can export these products, or cause them to be exported, or aid in the development of foreign markets.

To that end, the CCC had $26.8 billion invested in commodity loans and inventories as of September 30, 1987. Loans outstanding totaled $15.1 billion and inventories $11.7 billion. The inventories included wheat, corn, cotton, rice, and soybeans, along with 1.2 billion pounds of surplus dairy products, worth $1.4 billion, as a result of the CCC's price-supporting purchases of butter, cheese, and dried milk.

To manage the CCC's mounting inventory, storage, and handling costs alone added up to $1.4 billion in fiscal 1987 in rental payments to more than four thousand private storage facilities.

And in the last but certainly not least of its chores, the CCC made nearly $11.4 billion in fiscal 1987 in direct payments to farmers as a subsidy to their farm incomes.

Through the years, the CCC has used a variety of export programs. They include commercial credit guarantee programs, sales for the Food for Peace (PL 480) program, and payments of CCC-owned commodities as bonuses to exporters who agree to lower prices in selected foreign markets. The CCC even acquires some property in the process. It took title to a nightclub in the Middle East when an Egyptian grain importer defaulted on a CCC-guaranteed loan. Taxpayers ultimately had to cover that expense, however. The club, located in war-torn Beirut, Lebanon, was destroyed by a terrorist's bomb.

An Entitlement Program

Along with its ability to manipulate farm prices and exports, the CCC offers farm-state members of Congress a unique form of political power, which stems from this paradox: It is an "entitlement" program that must be funded through the regular appropriations process.

An entitlement is a federal program such as Social Security or unemployment compensation that guarantees a certain level of benefits to recipients who meet the requirements set by law. Once Congress establishes the eligibility criteria, it has no subsequent discretion on how much money the program will cost in any year. Almost all farm price-support programs financed by the CCC are entitlements. Farmers who meet the eligibility criteria are guaranteed full benefits. The more farmers eligible, the more money the CCC must spend on farm program benefits.

Disaster-relief programs provide aid to farmers who suffer weather-related crop failures. Pictured is an Iowa farmstead flooded by the Missouri River in 1952.

But the CCC cannot spend money like Social Security or unemployment compensation, which are independently funded through payroll taxes. The CCC is structured to give Congress a largely symbolic, yet consequential, hand in its annual spending authority.

The CCC borrows money from the Treasury and other lenders to finance its operations. Much of the CCC's expenditures involve loans to farmers and purchases of commodities. As farmers repay their loans and as CCC commodity stocks are sold, the CCC recovers funds and pays off its debts. But the CCC typically does not recover as much money as it spends. Sometimes there are big losses, such as when commodities are sold for prices lower than the CCC paid for them, or when it makes direct payments to support farmers' incomes. When it

94

realizes losses in its operations, the CCC must turn to Congress with a request for appropriations.

This method of funding, sometimes called "backdoor" financing, gives the CCC greater flexibility and freedom in spending federal money than normal agencies of government. It also protects farm programs from sudden changes in policy. Because the CCC contracts with farmers in one year, sometimes for loan payments to be made in the following year (and reimbursed in the year after that), Congress cannot break those contracts by making immediate changes in price-support programs. "It's a system that served the interests of agriculture," said Cochran. "Many other programs depend on the whim of Congress and the president. This has stabilized farm programs. There's a degree of certainty that producers have, that program payments will be made."

That protection extends even into the realm of congressional budget policy. During the long House-Senate negotiations in 1985 on Gramm-Rudman-Hollings, farm-state members of the House, led by Whitten, won a provision that exempted the CCC from any automatic budget reductions. The cash payments made directly to farmers were subject to the same, across-the-board cuts that other programs were, but as a result of Whitten's exemption for the CCC, the Agriculture Department found a way to get around reducing farmers' deficiency payments. They made the payments in the form of payment-in-kind (PIK) certificates, redeemable for CCC-owned grain. PIK certificates were not subject to Gramm-Rudman cuts.

Little Chance for Reform

The difficulty of reining in the CCC—and thus holding down farm program costs—continues to frustrate congressional budget writers. "Perhaps the time has come for us to do something as radical as 'de-entitle' farm programs, and put a cap on what the CCC is spending, so at least we know how much is going out," said Pete V. Domenici, the ranking Republican on the Senate Budget Committee. He then added that such an idea had no chance in Congress.

The slide in the farm economy and the unpredictably explosive changes in the cost of federal farm programs has highlighted another idiosyncrasy in CCC funding, one that makes it actually less flexible than other entitlement programs. Congress has placed a ceiling on how much the CCC can borrow—$30 billion, as of 1988. If the CCC reaches that cap, it loses further authority to borrow money. Unless Congress appropriates more money for the corporation to repay some of its debt to the Treasury, the CCC must shut down its entire operation. This is similar to the predicament the government faces when Congress fails to raise the ceiling on the national debt: The Treasury cannot borrow to pay off its maturing debts.

Until recently, the cap on CCC borrowing authority was rarely a problem. Each January when the president submitted a budget for the next fiscal year, the Agriculture Department would simply estimate how much money the CCC spent on farm programs, how much it made back, and then asked Congress to cover the difference. Congress routinely obliged by authorizing the requested appropriation. When CCC operations bumped up against the cap too often, Congress merely increased the ceiling.

But until late 1987, the last time Congress raised CCC's borrowing authority was in 1983, when the ceiling was lifted from $20 billion to $25 billion. In that time farm program costs shot up to record heights as more and more farmers signed up for price- and income-protection under the law. In addition, the Agriculture Department consistently fell short in its early predictions for the CCC's year-end losses. Even when Congress gave the CCC what the president requested in January, it was not enough to keep the corporation going through the full October-through-September fiscal year. "You're trying to estimate outlays before farmers have even planted a crop," said Richard Pazdalski, an Agriculture Department budget analyst.

Some see Whitten's hand in this predicament. By sticking with the president's original request for the CCC, even when it had already become apparent that it was far short of what the corporation would need, Whitten effectively forced the administration to come forward with a request for supplemental appropriations.

The Reagan administration tried repeatedly to take the CCC out of that merry-go-round with a proposal for a "permanent, indefinite" appropriation to reimburse the corporation's losses. That would allow it to draw as much money as it needed from the Treasury without ever returning to Congress for new spending authority—in other words, it would become a true entitlement program. In 1987 the administration also asked Congress to lift the ceiling on the CCC's borrowing authority from $25 billion to $40 billion, so that even if Congress insisted on keeping tabs on the CCC by requiring the administration to request annual appropriations, the agency could keep on functioning. It could simply borrow more money from the Treasury.

For years Congress—and particularly Whitten—persistently refused even to consider either idea. Whitten maintained that the current system of limited appropriations was the only way Congress could keep an eye on agriculture spending. He also complained that the administration used the CCC to fund a number of programs that did not involve price supports and export sales, which he believed should be the sole purposes of the corporation.

In many respects, Whitten was right. Non-price-support programs that were funded through the CCC in fiscal 1987 and 1988 included crop insurance, a conservation reserve program, a whole-herd dairy buyout program, red meat purchases for schools and the military, and special subsidies for ethanol plants. "They're paying all this through CCC, because we took the strings off it [in Gramm-Rudman]," Whitten said. "We took them off for particular purposes, to support prices and exports. But they're using [the CCC] for anything they don't want to count."

Cochran tried to find a middle ground between Whitten and the administration. He won Senate passage in past years for a variation on the administration's proposal, called a "current, indefinite" appropriation for the CCC. This would give the CCC unlimited reimbursements on a year-by-year basis and free it from the midyear ritual of a supplemental. But even fellow Mississippian Cochran got nowhere with Whitten. "It's not just a philosophical tug of war," Cochran said. "What it boils down to is, this is a necessary piece of legislation that the Appropriations Committee gets to write at least once a year."

The New Kid on the Block

Enter Patrick J. Leahy, Democrat of Vermont and the new kid on the block in the congressional power structure for agriculture. Late in 1987, the relatively new chairman of the Senate Agriculture Committee dared to take on the leader of the pack and got a hard lesson in farm-state street politics.

The controversy, as usual, involved an appropriations bill for agriculture, for fiscal 1988, which had been wrapped into a

In 1987, the relatively new chairman of the Senate Agriculture Committee, Patrick J. Leahy, D-Vt., got a hard lesson in farm-state street politics.

governmentwide spending bill known as a continuing resolution. This time, however, the crucial conflict was not so much between Senate and House Appropriations committees as it was between Whitten and the regular Agriculture committees.

Members of the House and Senate Agriculture committees plainly had come to resent Whitten's intrusion into their policy domain. His ability to control CCC funding and occasionally tie up farm program payments for weeks, while he engaged in hardball political standoffs with the Reagan administration, had begun to wear on farm-state politicians outside Whitten's own subcommittee. The Agriculture panel members believed they were being unfairly blamed by farmer-constituents when, in their minds, Whitten was actually at fault for CCC checks being held up.

Late in 1987 House Agriculture Committee chairman E. "Kika" de la Garza tried to challenge Whitten's control over the CCC on the House floor. But when it became apparent that his House colleagues were not about to challenge the powerful Appropriations chairman over an obscure and esoteric farm issue, de la Garza caved in. On turf questions involving the CCC and appropriations law, Whitten clearly ruled the House.

So, instead, it was left to Leahy and his Senate panel to take on Whitten. Leahy tried to force Whitten's hand by putting the indefinite funding mechanism for the CCC into two Senate bills that Whitten would have no voice on when they came over to the House—the Senate's comprehensive trade bill and the Senate's fiscal 1988 deficit-reduction, or "reconciliation," bill. Bolstering Leahy and his Senate Agriculture colleagues was a well-publicized White House-congressional budget "summit" agreement, where all participants vowed to avoid supplemental appropriations in 1988, except in "dire emergencies."

Not to be outdone in legislative legerdemain, the wily Whitten fought back. Instead of allocating the CCC's $21 billion appropriation request in a lump sum, as was the usual practice, his appropriations bill for fiscal 1989 would distribute funds among various CCC programs, providing $6.1 billion for income-supports payments, $5.1 billion for loans, and so on. The restrictions on how the CCC could spend its money would be even more severe than in the past.

Upon seeing this language, apopleptic administration officials howled that Whitten's new funding method would force the CCC to shut down within weeks and require a supplemental appropriation before the ink was dry on the continuing resolution. So on December 16, Leahy and an entourage of Senate Agriculture Committee aides hustled over to the House-Senate agriculture conference on the continuing resolution and prepared to square off with Whitten.

Leahy got nowhere with the recalcitrant Appropriations chairman. Whitten obviously controlled every vote in the House delegation, and Cochran, in the GOP minority on the Senate side, had little leverage to negotiate with him because his Democratic counterparts on the Senate Appropriations panel were not that interested in challenging Whitten. Finally Leahy was reduced to begging. "We can't do it that way, Jamie," he said, to little avail.

Cochran, who had fought the CCC funding battle with Whitten many times in the past, to similarly unsuccessful results, said he nevertheless agreed with Whitten's main complaint that the Agriculture committees had abused the CCC's "revolving" account to pay for programs that should be appropriated individually. Cochran eventually worked out a deal with Whitten that kept the House language but also allowed the CCC more flexibility in tranferring money from one account to another. And in an even more significant move, Whitten agreed to raise the CCC's borrowing authority from $25 billion to $30 billion, a change that could do more than anything to avoid the need for CCC supplemental appropriations in the near future.

But even Cochran conceded that instead of getting closer to the Senate's preferred indefinite funding method, he and Leahy were forced to backpeddle. Whitten's guileful move to clamp down more strongly on CCC appropriations effectively forced the senators to defend the existing definite-appropriations funding procedure they had long tried to get rid of. "I guess we were hoping you wouldn't notice," Cochran said sheepishly.

Leahy, however, was not quite ready to give up his quest. With the help of Senate Budget Committee leaders, he pressed for approval of the indefinite-funding authority for the CCC in the reconciliation bill. Without it, he argued, the understanding reached at the summit to avoid supplementals could easily unravel. Since the House-Senate conference on the reconciliation bill did not include Whitten, it went through with little notice. On the same day that Congress ultimately approved Whitten's more conventional appropriations measure, it also passed Leahy's new CCC funding method in the reconciliation bill.

When President Reagan signed the two budget bills in reverse order, making reconciliation the last to be enacted into law, some Senate staffers argued hopefully that the indefinite funding mechanism would override Whitten's restrictive appropriation for the CCC. But officials at the Agriculture Department quickly dashed those expectations. They said that Leahy's provision could not take effect until fiscal 1989, if then. Department officials said they were bound by the appropriating language, which, in the parlance of federal lawmaking, took precedence over the reconciliation bill's less mandatory authorizing language.

"In effect, Congress was writing itself a memo in the reconciliation bill," said Steven B. Dewhurst, director of the Agriculture Department's budget office. "But Congress didn't follow that. It approved a provision [for definite appropriations], and that's the law." Dewhurst said only natural and economic forces could forestall a need for a CCC supplemental before the fiscal year ended in September 1988. No amount of legislative or statutory sleight of hand could prevent it.

In other words, the CCC would still be subject to the vagaries of the farm economy and the weather. Sudden changes in prices or production could drive the costs of farm programs well beyond expectations, forcing the administration to return to Congress with a supplemental funding request, just as it had in five of the previous six years.

Leahy sought an independent ruling from the comptroller general of the United States, but he, too, concluded that Whitten's line-item appropriations for the CCC were not nullified by reconciliation language. Yet the situation could be different in 1989, the comptroller's office said. The reconciliation bill actually requires the Appropriations committees to follow the indefinite funding method in future appropriations for the CCC, a technicality that could eventually tie Whitten's hands. "It could set up a floor fight during next year's budget cycle," said John Podesta, a legal aide to Leahy.

But the question remained whether Congress would choose to abandon the convenience of the "must-pass" CCC supplemental. The turf battle between Leahy and Whitten may seem inconsequential by comparison. "They may have overplayed their hand," observed Whitten's protégé Traxler. "Mr. Whitten is not going to allow some upstart who just got off the train to come in and mess with his favorite programs."

The Ideas behind the Power

As wily and cynical as Whitten's legislative style and tactics may seem, not all of what he does with the CCC is pure political power grabbing. Underlying his actions on behalf of agriculture spending is a longstanding, if somewhat singleminded, commitment to U.S. farmers.

Whitten, for his part, tries to play down his authoritarian image. In a wide-ranging interview in mid-1987, he portrayed himself as just a country philosopher who thinks mostly about the big picture, which to him is the U.S. economy, as framed by federal farm policy.

"My job is to protect the economy of the country," he said. It was preface to a familiar theme with Whitten: that agriculture is one of three cornerstones of the nation's power and wealth. The other two he calls "labor" and "industry." And agriculture, he likes to say, affects "84 percent of the geography" of this country.

"I say again," he said, "if labor goes down, the country will go down. If our industry goes down, the country will go down. What they don't see is that if you let agriculture go down, it'll pull the others down. You say it won't happen? Well, we've got a federal deficit of $170 billion. For the first time since 1914, we're a debtor nation. . . . Don't tell me it won't pull [the nation] down. It *has* pulled it down."

Whitten believes that the fifty-year-old structure of federal farm policy was intended to protect that delicate balance. And, indeed, many close observers of Whitten believe he is best revealed in the context of those programs created in his political infancy. "He's probably the last New Dealer left on Capitol Hill," said Richard J. Durbin, an Illinois Democrat and a member of Whitten's subcommittee. "He believes firmly in pump priming. He's seen what that's meant.

"One thing I marvel at," added Durbin, who was born three years after Whitten was first elected to Congress. "That man was sitting on the House floor on the day FDR gave his 'Day of Infamy' speech," which sent the country into World War II.

Mississippi's deep poverty in the Great Depression, and its resurgence during and after World War II, have left a lasting impression on Whitten's political thinking. "Now lots of folks can tell you why we had a depression," he said. "But few can tell why it took 10 years to get over it. And when they did begin to get over it, it was when the first farm program, under Roosevelt, was enacted."

As in Mississippi, the economic woes of the entire South were compounded by a lack of commercial resources. "For many years, we just didn't have the capital," Whitten said. "In much of the South, you borrowed money from Memphis, and Memphis from St. Louis, and St. Louis from New York. Until the government got into it, there just wasn't enough capital for development. I make no apologies for federal programs. Because when we put the federal government in is when our rural areas quickly became wealthy."

Whitten's concept of wealth is central to his approach to government, and to agriculture. He believes a nation's wealth is measured by its physical assets, not by its money. With that in mind, he won those important CCC exemptions from Gramm-Rudman. "The farmer is the caretaker of the fertility of our soil," he said. "We're having all these arguments about Gramm-Rudman and these [spending] limits. [But] you can't let soil conservation go, reforestry go, watershed protection, harbors—that's your real wealth. The mistake about Gramm-Rudman is, you're trying to handle your paper money, but your real wealth goes down the drain.... And let me repeat again, since we started meeting local problems with federal programs in 1934, our wealth has increased 41 percent. I mean real wealth," he went on, warming to another opportunity to expound his fiscal viewpoint. "Money's not wealth. It's just a medium of exchange."

Much of Whitten's energy is spent defending the agricultural legacies of the New Deal—the Rural Electrification Administration, the Soil Conservation Service, the Farmers Home Administration, and the CCC—programs that he believes brought new opportunities to the rural South. Despite having more seniority on the Appropriations Committee than any other subcommittee chairman, Whitten has chosen to keep the Agriculture post instead of switching to another subcommittee. "It's not a whole lot of glamour to it," he said. "But I'm proud to have my name on rural electricity, water systems, telephones, high service roads in 84 percent of this country."

And in 1987 this son of a Mississippi farmer made his

influence felt throughout rural Michigan as well. In response to the pleas of Traxler and other members, Whitten won House approval for an extra $135 million for the disaster-relief program, enough to cover flood losses everywhere. As was his habit, Whitten attached the money to a supplemental appropriations measure required to keep the CCC operating. Compared with $6.7 billion for the CCC or other large items, the disaster money was practically hidden from view.

In creating his opportunities, Whitten has learned how to get what he wants by making it possible for others to get what they want. It is a political equation he says he learned in his early law days in Mississippi, where his mentors were his law

"Permanent secretary of agriculture" Jamie L. Whitten formed his ideas on farm policy in the midst of the Great Depression. Pictured above, the National Guard holds a protesting crowd in check at an Iowa farm foreclosure sale in 1933.

partner, a prosecutor, and a local judge. "The judge was the one that said, 'Jamie, all anybody wants is a fair advantage,' " Whitten said. "And I added to that: the way to get a fair advantage is to pass a law declaring it fair. And that's what all laws are about. . . . That's the contest that goes on around here all the time."

Asked if he had not won more than his share of those contests, Whitten smiled wryly. "Well, I've had a whole lot of fun."

Chapter 6

Debt Crisis

Once upon a time, a farm-state politician could fawn shamelessly over an obscure and rather arcane institution called the Farm Credit System. Back in the 1950s and 1960s, for instance, Sen. Allen Joseph Ellender was known to wax metaphorically about this nationwide network of agricultural lenders. "Our blue-eyed, blond-haired girl in pigtails and pinafore" was an image the powerful Appropriations Committee chairman liked to repeat, as if Congress's well-behaved progeny needed little watchful protection. Veteran representative Ed Jones, Democratic member—and later chairman—of the House Agriculture Subcommittee on Credit, recalled a similar sentiment from his early days on Capitol Hill. "We called it the 'sweetheart of Congress,'" he said. "No problems."

The Farm Credit System had that kind of effect on federal lawmakers. As a creature of Congress, founded in 1916, it grew into a government enterprise that worked. Its banks provided cheap loans to family farmers, who were the owners and directors of their own lending cooperatives. Together they paid the government back and even turned a hefty profit.

But the romance began to sour in 1985, when the system reported its first financial losses since the Great Depression. A total of nearly $5 billion in losses over two years and the prospect of going $3 billion deeper into debt by 1989 prompted system officials to come to Capitol Hill for help. Unless Congress ponied up $6 billion, they said, much of the system would go bankrupt, posing the politically abhorrent possibility of uprooting the farm economy and, worse, wreaking havoc on the nation's entire financial system. The rescue promised to cost far

Rep. Ed Jones, D-Tenn., recalled that members referred to the Farm Credit System as "the 'sweetheart of Congress.'"

more than the New York City and Chrysler bailouts of the 1970s. In an era of $150 billion annual federal deficits, Congress had no room in its budget for that kind of profligate expenditure.

Nevertheless, the main question throughout 1987 was not whether the government would step in, but how and when. Members of Congress and the Reagan administration agreed that the political and economic risks associated with the system's downfall were too great to ignore. And after struggling for the better part of the year with this complex financial crisis, Congress passed landmark legislation to rescue and reorganize the ailing Farm Credit System. The bill sailed through both the House and Senate by overwhelming margins. In January 1988 President Reagan signed the bill, providing up to $4 billion in financial assistance to failing system banks. Congress even found a creative way to raise the money through new bond issues, so that most of the rescue cash would not have to come straight from the Treasury.

Ultimately, however, the government itself would be responsible for the bailout expense if system banks proved unable to repay the bonds.

Yet Congress, in the process of reaffirming its protective role over the system, went well beyond a simple rescue. It took big steps to broaden the government's hand in providing ready and affordable credit to all of the nation's farmers, not just those borrowers of the Farm Credit System. System banks were given strict new rules for keeping as many of their borrowers afloat as possible. But Congress also bound the federal Farmers Home Administration (FmHA), an Agriculture Department agency known as the "lender of last resort" for farmers who could not get credit elsewhere, to the same obligation to provide "borrower rights" and protections against foreclosure. The measure effectively ended an eight-year campaign by the Reagan administration to weed out the more questionable accounts in the FmHA's portfolio.

Moreover, Congress made a potentially far-reaching bow to commercial banks and insurance companies, which compete with Farm Credit System institutions for borrowers. The bailout bill established a new, federally supported secondary market for trading securities backed by fixed-rate farm real estate loans. The secondary market—dubbed "Farmer Mac" after similar creations for home loans—was bolstered by a $1.5

billion "line of credit" from the Treasury, giving private lenders a leg up to offer loans at interest rates low enough to be competitive with system banks.

As the scope of the legislation began to unfold, members became increasingly aware of its wider implications—namely, increased federal involvement in all forms of farm lending. "In effect," said Glenn English of the House Agriculture Committee, voicing what no one else seemed anxious to admit, "we're going to federalize every darn farm loan in this country."

An Explosion of Farm Debt

Farmers in the United States have always relied on credit to make ends meet. The nature of their business, which requires them to invest time and money early in the year in expectation of a return many months later, encouraged farmers to look at cheap money and easy credit as simple tools of their trade. They needed credit to develop and expand their farms—to buy fertilizer, heavy equipment, and other necessary supplies that they could not produce for themselves—and they found it easier to pay off their debts with inflated product prices than with constant or falling product prices. As a result they looked to the federal government to promote liberal banking laws, weak banking regulations, and an expanded money supply, which they believed would keep prices moving upward. (See Figure 6-1.)

Even so, agriculture was largely a cash-financed industry before World War II. The inherent risks associated with farming only fueled farmers' existing Old World suspicions about going too deeply into debt. Not until the mid-1950s and the emergence of growth-oriented farm operations did farmers become highly motivated to expand their holdings through the intensive use of credit. Since then there has been an explosion of farm debt at least half of which was made available through federal lenders, "often at subsidized rates," according to University of California-Davis economist Lawrence Shepard. Farm borrowing increased five-fold between 1950 and 1980, with the largest part incurred by a small proportion of relatively aggressive, expansion-oriented farmers. Moreover, the prices farmers received for their crops generally could not support the interest rates they were paying on their loans. "Agriculture borrowers were largely driven by speculative motives associated with holding land, rather than by the operating income it generated,"

"In effect," said Glenn English, Democrat from Oklahoma and member of the House Agriculture Committee, "we're going to federalize every darn farm loan in this country."

Figure 6-1 Farm Debt

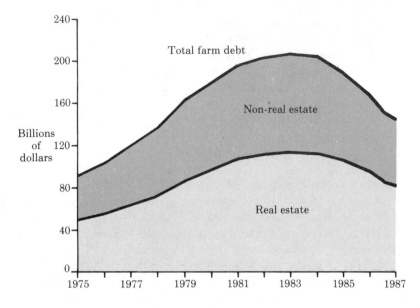

Source: U.S. Department of Agriculture, Economic Research Service, *Agricultural Finance,* April 1988.

Note: Farm loans outstanding December 31, 1986.

Shepard said in 1985.

The crisis spawned by the growth in farm debt in the United States went hand in hand with the problems of agriculture in general during the 1980s, and with land values in particular. "There is, as might be expected, a marked relationship between farm prosperity and depression and the value of farm land," agricultural historian Wayne D. Rasmussen has written. In prosperous times farmers tend to overborrow, using their land as security. Then in depressed times those land values fall, leaving less to back up loans and prompting calls "to make more loan funds available, to extend periods of payment, to negotiate forgiveness of some percentage of the loans, or to legislate moratoriums on foreclosures."

Congress to the Rescue

The federal government was a willing partner in the effort to secure affordable credit and more lenient terms for farmers.

Like most other U.S. farm programs, agricultural credit programs blossomed during the depression era between World War I and World War II. American farmers had just come through a period of unprecedented increases in prices, incomes, and land values when the United States became a major exporter of grains to war-torn Europe.

But that boomtime was followed by more than twenty years of decline in the real value of farmland, causing severe problems for farmers trying to repay their debts. Widespread rural bank failures followed, and lenders in general began to shy away from agriculture, making the supply of loanable funds to farmers either unreliable or available only at very high interest rates and restrictive terms.

Recognizing a shortage of farm credit at a time when nearly half of the population lived in rural areas, Congress came to the rescue. It established a number of new programs designed to reduce the risk of farming—for example, the price-support programs. In addition, Congress made a point of getting farmers better access to credit—hence the current panoply of easy-lending programs sponsored by the federal government. Three principle institutions were created to administer these programs: the Commodity Credit Corporation (CCC), the Farmers Home Administration and its predecessor agencies, and the banks of the Farm Credit System.

The CCC mainly provides loans to farmers at harvest so they can hold their crops off the market in hopes of getting a better price later in the year. Its intended function is to stabilize the prices of major commodities during periods of high and low supply.

The Farm Credit System and the FmHA, on the other hand, were designed to provide loans to farmers to buy land and to pay for the operating expenses of putting a crop in the ground. The loans they offered to farmers served as a means for the government to rectify what had become known as a "credit gap" for many agricultural producers, who had been unable to get loans from private credit markets. Indeed, farmers' access to credit was a problem long before the development of federal farm programs in the early part of the twentieth century. "During the whole of our colonial period and the first century of our national life," noted one writer in 1932, "financing the farmers was one of our major economic programs, playing a larger part in politics than any other question except those of slavery and the tariff."

The federal government also had an important social objective behind the push to maintain a steady flow of affordable credit to farmers and ranchers in the hinterland. During the early 1900s farmers had experienced great difficulty buying good farm land, and government officials were alarmed by a large rise in farm tenancy. Even creditworthy farmers could not get long-term financing to buy land. Most of the nation's money centers were concentrated on the East Coast, and small country banks offered only loans that came due in two to five years. If farmers suffered one drought year, they would be unable to make their payments, and the bank would take their land away.

As farmers' political influence began to build in Washington, President Theodore Roosevelt in 1908 created the Country Life Commission to study how the government could help farmers obtain credit. That study and others that followed resulted in a push for a land-bank system, based on a Scandinavian model, to be organized as a borrower-owned cooperative. The government would provide the start-up money through a special bond issue, and farmer-borrowers would be required to buy stock in their local associations to help the system pay off its government loan.

And in fact, the Farm Credit System, founded in 1916 and recapitalized in the 1930s, would eventually pay off the last of its government loans in 1968. Yet this system, as such, was actually a confederation of regional money centers and local lending associations, without a central decision-making authority. Its decentralized structure has always been a fiercely protected feature, since each lending association and each bank could control its own destiny.

Like the Federal Reserve, which Congress created about the same time as the first components of the Farm Credit System, the confederation was divided into twelve regions of the country. Each district contained a self-supporting federal land bank for real estate loans and a self-supporting federal intermediate credit bank for shorter-term production loans, plus a bank for cooperatives. Real estate and operating loans were made to farmers through local land bank associations and production credit associations run by farmers.

Since the system's founding, the mission of federal agricultural credit programs has been as much social and political as economic. The Farmers Home Administration took the objec-

tives begun by the Farm Credit System one step further, to the point where it has become the lead federal agency for providing financial and technical assistance to farmers and rural communities. The lineage of Farmers Home traces to Franklin Roosevelt's Resettlement Administration of 1935, when its primary mission was to provide loans and assistance to depression-stricken farm families. In 1946, Congress reorganized and renamed the agency and gave it new authority to insure loans made by banks, other agencies, and private individuals as well as to provide direct government loans.

The early years of the Farmers Home Administration and its predecessors were focused on the chronic poverty of U.S. farm families. Its main function was to keep many of them on the land and, it was hoped, at least partly stem the huge tide of rural migration into the cities. The government went out of its way to entice families to stay on the farm. Until the late 1970s, interest rates charged by the FmHA on farmer program loans did not even cover changes in the government's own cost of funds—that is, the interest rate on ninety-day Treasury bills. Congress eventually expanded the FmHA's role and authority

The crisis spawned by the growth in farm debt in the United States went hand in hand with the problems of agriculture in general during the 1980s, and with land values in particular.

111

to provide credit to rural communities and nonfarm rural families for housing, water, and waste disposal projects.

Over the years, however, a subtle shift occurred in the goals of FmHA credit assistance. The original welfare mission gave way to other objectives. Ronald Meekhof of the Agriculture Department's Economic Research Service noted that the depression-era goal of maintaining low-income, self-sufficient farms was gradually replaced by an effort to foster commercially viable enterprises. Land loans shifted in emphasis, away from financing farm purchases by a tenant and toward helping current owners enlarge and develop their operations. FmHA credit policy also moved toward providing credit to all farmers who for various reasons were unable to obtain credit elsewhere. Both subsistence farmers and large commercial operators were eligible to get loans from the FmHA if they could not find it from commercial lenders at reasonable terms.

Debt Shares

Together the Farm Credit System and the Farmers Home Administration changed the structure of U.S. agriculture. The new flow of money and other capital resources into agriculture financed agriculture's technological revolution between the 1930s and 1970s. These lending institutions were so effective that by the 1960s and into the 1970s and 1980s farmers were getting easier access to loans and at lower interest rates than any other sector of the nation's economy, according to some studies. In 1983, the CCC and FmHA were the federal pipelines for distributing $17.8 billion in direct loans to farmers—41 percent of all such transactions by the government, according to the Agriculture Department. New lending by the Farm Credit System, meanwhile, amounted to about $50 billion a year, or 30 percent of all lending by government-sponsored agencies. Federal and federally related agencies held 52 percent of the farm real estate debt outstanding and 44 percent of non-real estate debt.

A closer look at the share of farm debt held by government and government-sponsored agencies shows the impact these institutions had on agriculture through the 1970s and gives a hint of the financial and political problems they would experience in the 1980s.

As of January 1984, the Farm Credit System alone accounted for 32 percent of all farm debt outstanding. Commercial banks held 22 percent, while individuals and other private lenders, such as merchants and supply dealers, held 24 percent. Life insurance companies, which have played an important (though declining) role in farm lending, held only a 6 percent share by 1984. Government lenders—the FmHA, the CCC, and the Small Business Administration—accounted for about 12 percent, 5 percent, and 1 percent of farm sector debt, respectively.

Dividing farm debt into real estate and non-real estate categories—land loans as opposed to debts incurred for operating expenses—further illustrates how changes in market shares of farm debt have occurred over the years. The Farm Credit System's share of all farm real estate loans increased steadily since 1960, from only 19 percent to a high of 44 percent on January 1, 1984. This occurred for a variety of reasons, including the system's ability to offer lower average interest rates than other lenders, its availability of loan funds and specialization in farm real estate debt, and the liberalization of its lending policies in 1971 and 1980. In essence, the system's federal land banks were not subject to the same periodic shortages of credit faced by commercial banks. (See Table 6-1.)

Life insurance companies were once heavily involved in real estate debt markets. Their market share peaked at 25 percent in the late 1950s but declined steadily to only 11 percent by 1984. This was largely the result of an increase in demand for policyholder loans, increased returns from nonfarm investments, and restrictive state usury laws.

Commercial banks, on the other hand, have never been active in the farm real estate debt market. Most of the liabilities of banks are short term, which means they have little interest in long-term lending. Since 1960 banks have held an average of 12 percent to 13 percent of all farm real estate debt, and that share fell after 1980 to around 8 percent. This relatively small decline had significant implications, however; a principal battle in the system's rescue bill was an attempt by commercial banks to regain their share of the farm real estate debt market.

In non-real estate debt, commercial banks and the Farm Credit System's production credit associations (PCAs) have been clearly dominant lenders. Commercial banks' debt share increased steadily from 1962, when they held 36 percent of all farm non-real estate debt, until it peaked in 1974 at 51 percent.

Table 6-1 Market Shares of Real Estate Farm Debt, 1960-1987

Year	Farm Credit System	Farmers Home Administration	Life insurance companies	Commercial banks	Individuals and others
1960	19%	6%	23%	13%	39%
1961	20	6	23	12	39
1962	20	7	23	12	38
1963	20	7	23	12	38
1964	20	7	22	12	38
1965	20	7	23	13	38
1966	20	7	23	13	38
1967	21	7	23	12	37
1968	22	7	22	12	36
1969	22	7	21	12	37
1970	23	8	20	12	38
1971	24	8	19	12	38
1972	25	8	17	13	37
1973	26	8	16	14	36
1974	28	8	15	14	36
1975	30	7	14	13	35
1976	32	7	14	13	35
1977	34	7	13	12	34
1978	34	6	14	12	34
1979	35	6	15	12	33
1980	35	8	14	10	33
1981	38	8	14	9	32
1982	41	8	12	8	30
1983	43	8	12	8	29
1984	43	8	11	8	29
1985	44	9	11	9	27
1986	42	10	11	11	26
1987	40	11	12	13	25

Source: U.S. Department of Agriculture, Economic Research Service.

Note: As of January 1.

It settled back down to about a third of the market share by 1987. The market share of PCAs also increased during the 1960s, rising from only 10 percent to as much as 26 percent in 1976. Their share also has fallen in the 1980s, however, to less than 20 percent.

Since the mid-1970s, both commercial banks and PCAs lost market shares to government lenders, the FmHA, and the CCC, as below-market rates for government farm lending apparently reduced the demand for private farm credit. The role of Farmers Home increased substantially after 1977 when Congress expanded its emergency loan programs. Its share of non-real estate debt grew from 5 percent of the market to 15 percent as a direct result. Congressionally mandated "disaster" loans also showed a phenomenal rise, growing from $2 billion in 1978 to $10 billion in 1983.

Good Times, Bad Times

Against this shifting backdrop of increasing government lending and decreasing private lender involvement, the Farm Credit System went on to rack up unprecedented profits during the 1970s. Its gains were based largely on soaring farmland values—jacked up by export-driven farm prices—and were helped by legislation that liberalized the system's lending powers. In 1971 Congress passed a law allowing system banks to make loans equal to 85 percent of the appraised value of the farmland offered as collateral. Before then, bank officers could lend up to only 65 percent of the "normal agricultural value" of real estate—an important distinction, since speculative land values were skyrocketing far beyond the return farmers were used to getting for their production.

Many banks took advantage of this new wrinkle in the law to aggressively market bigger loans to farmers. Thousands of farmers, recognizing a potential for big windfall profits from their rising land values, willingly played along and began taking out more and bigger loans, which, as it turned out, they could not pay back from the cash income they were getting for their crops. Farmers' collateral was merely the speculative value of the land.

The system also found a way to corner the market, offering relatively low interest rates during a period of high inflation. Unlike commercial banks, which make loans based for the most part on the money they take in from depositors, Farm Credit System institutions do not take deposits. They raise capital by selling bonds and discount notes on corporate securities markets. The bonds were aided by the system's quasi-public status as a federally sponsored institution, which made the notes seem even more secure and allowed system officials to price them at even lower interest rates than other, highly rated private sector bonds. During the 1970s, even as interest rates on new bond issues were rising, system banks could still afford to charge farmers far lower rates than commercial lenders. They could base loan rates not on their most recent bond issues, but on the average cost of all their outstanding debts—which were, of course, dominated by the lower interest rates of the previous decade.

But the full weight of a sodden farm economy fell hard on the thirty-seven money centers and seven hundred local associations that made up the system's lending network. When inflation and interest rates dropped in the 1980s, they were caught by their own gambit, leaving many banks as victims of their own success.

Suddenly, private commercial lenders could significantly undercut system banks, whose outstanding bond obligations were now dominated by higher-priced issues. At the same time, export prices for farm products tumbled and U.S. farmland values followed suit. Farmers holding mortgages with system banks were increasingly unable to meet their payments, and if the struggling lenders sought to foreclose, the sinking value of the land would not cover the cost of the mortgages.

As a result, the system was left holding a bundle of bad debts. By 1987, nearly one-fourth of the system's dwindling, $55 billion loan portfolio consisted of questionable-to-failing loans. Though system banks still held one-quarter of the estimated $186 billion in total U.S. farm debt—and nearly half of the nation's agricultural real estate loans—the most creditworthy borrowers were fleeing to other commercial lenders in droves.

A number of system lenders were left with such negligible assets that eleven major system institutions declared they were in danger of going bankrupt by the end of 1987. The entire system had a remaining surplus of only $1.2 billion, not enough to cover the projected losses of faltering banks. Capital reserves included another $4 billion in stock that farmer-borrowers were required to buy when they took out loans. But many of the system's best borrowers, fearful that their stock would be used to cover the system's losses, began paying off their loans and leaving the system.

The fact that twenty-six of the thirty-seven banks were still profitable—and at the same time liable for the debts of the weaker banks—was in itself a large part of the system's problem. The decentralized structure was a fiercely protected feature of the system, since each lending association and bank could control its own destiny. But it also bred suspicion and turmoil among different institutions, largely along regional lines.

Banks in healthier districts on the East Coast and in Texas, where land values had not slid the way they did in the Midwest, South, and Far West, still were obliged under law to use much of their profits to bolster the sagging fortunes of their weaker sisters. In response, the healthy banks complained openly about past foibles and mismanagement in the recipient institutions. Officials in the weaker districts, forced to cope with record defaults, also came in for bitter attacks from their own farmer-borrowers for their allegedly arrogant management styles and strict loan-collection practices. "You can't go out and collect a million loans and maintain your reputation as Mr. Nice Guy," acknowledged H. Brent Beesley, president of the Farm Credit Corporation of America, which represents the system's managers and directors.

All this contributed to a real public relations problem for the system. Rent by internal dissension and lacking a central authority, bank officials could not present a unified voice when seeking congressional help. "There is a babble of voices here that's contributed to the loss of confidence," said Ed Jaenke, a former governor of the system.

Foregone Conclusion

Operating under these clouds of a depressed economy and a worsening public image, system officials in 1987 marched up Capitol Hill for the third time in as many years with dire warnings of the institution's imminent demise.

Congress had been asked twice before to shore up its ailing progeny, and each time managed to avoid spending any hard cash. A 1985 measure significantly restructured the system, set up a program for loss-sharing among the various districts, and strengthened the powers of the Farm Credit Administration, the federal regulatory agency in charge of overseeing the system's operations. The 1985 bill also authorized direct financial assistance but required the system to apply for it through a separate appropriation.

But in 1986, when it appeared such assistance might be necessary for some banks, Congress again sidestepped the issue. Agriculture Committee members instead came up with a plan to loosen the system's accounting requirements. In effect, the law allowed the system to keep two sets of books to report their financial condition—one set showing actual earnings and losses, another taking current losses and spreading them out over twenty years. It was no less than what other, less legitimate enterprises call "creative accounting."

Less than three months after the law was passed, however, system officials were back on Capitol Hill. They insisted they would need a minimum of $6 billion directly from the Treasury to remain solvent. Wary farm-state lawmakers were not very happy to see them again but generally conceded that, this time, Congress probably would have to pay up.

Yet the widely held assumption that a federal rescue for the system was inevitable did nothing to clear a path for Congress to make it occur. At the beginning of 1987, Democratic leaders promised quick action on farm credit rescue legislation. Little happened. So many intertwining threads had begun to run through the subject that House and Senate Agriculture panels were virtually paralyzed for most of the year in their efforts to get a bill moving.

The legislative fast track was muddied by technical financial questions, tough budget negotiations, partisan maneuvering, and internecine committee battles. Much of the debate centered on questions such as how to protect the original mission of the system itself, which was to help farmers in every region of the country get credit to buy land. But since the system was one of the country's largest banking institutions, its fate also touched the financial underpinnings of the entire nation.

At first the problem was carried principally by farm-state members; they were splintered by their regional and crop-oriented differences. But as the budgetary and banking implications of the question began to loom, urban members weighed in—making a consensus solution seem even more elusive. "It's got to be done so that it doesn't break our bank," said Rep. Charles E. Schumer, Democrat from New York, a member of the House Budget Committee, and a frequent critic of high-cost farm programs. But even Schumer conceded that "the question is not *if*, but *how* it will be done."

Some members of Congress and the Reagan administration continued to challenge the high price tag. Administration officials maintained that it would be possible, through a variety of fund-raising methods, to limit the actual cost of a bailout and delay most of the actual outlays for two to three years. Some lawmakers, remembering that the system made similar forecasts of doom in each of the past two years—only to come up with ways to avoid federal spending—were skeptical that 1987 was really going to be the year of reckoning. "A lot of members want to see if the system is still crying wolf," said Rep. Fred Grandy, a Republican from Iowa.

Still, hardly anyone in Washington questioned the basic assumption that Congress eventually would step in to save the system. That was largely because of its strong economic and political ties to the government. The system had a long history of providing affordable credit to all kinds of farmers and farm-related businesses—key constituencies to both Democrats and Republicans—particularly preceding a presidential election year. The system also played a critical role in the nation's investment markets.

Taken together, the influence of both farmer and investor gave the system a broad-based constituency that extended from the little town of Wall, S.D., to the major financial houses of Wall Street. Even the Reagan administration, which had resisted the system's push for financial assistance in the past, conceded that some form of government bailout was obligatory. "The administration wants to keep the Farm Credit System there," said Charles O. Sethness, assistant Treasury secretary and the administration's point man on the issue. "We do not want to reverse 75 years of history."

Banking Issues Unfamiliar

In Congress, the system fell under the sole jurisdiction of the Agriculture committees, and much of the delay in moving legislation could be traced to the lack of expertise that their farm-oriented members brought to what was, at bottom, a banking issue. Rural lawmakers, used to forging working coalitions on the highly specialized and complex subject of farm price supports, were hard-pressed to fashion even small alliances to deal with the sophisticated problems of a large financial institution. "We don't know what's going on, because we're not bankers," admitted an aide to Edward R. Madigan of Illinois, ranking Republican on the House Agriculture Committee.

Also, Agriculture Committee members were more used to programs that gave cash directly from government to farmer. The prospect of jumping to the rescue of an impersonal banking organization did not inspire many members to quick action.

119

"There's almost no good politics in this thing," said an aide to Jones of the House Subcommittee on Credit. "You're talking about spending money, and essentially, you're talking about bailing out a lender. Nobody's in love with their lender."

But farm-state legislators' fondness for spending money on farmers created a political conflict with the Reagan administration, which viewed a system rescue package in a much colder light. "This isn't a farm program," complained Treasury's Sethness. "It's supposed to be, when it's run right, a privately run financial institution."

The Reagan administration said its solution would ensure that the system would maintain private status and never again return to the federal till. One way of accomplishing that, said Sethness, was to allow regional banks to compete with each other for customers—a kind of survival of the fittest that would gradually weed out the banks unable to make it on their own. "Many banks have been sitting there doing absolutely nothing to help themselves, waiting for the government check to arrive," Sethness said.

Democratic leaders in the House and Senate were working on the cost issue from a different angle, trying to find ways to justify up to $6 billion in new spending for agriculture at a time when price-support costs were expected to top $25 billion for the second year in a row. The concern over a possible urban backlash against increased farm spending prompted several farm commodity groups to take a new interest in the Farm Credit System rescue efforts. The administration had threatened these groups with steep cutbacks in their bread-and-butter programs, mainly farm price supports, to cover the expense of a system bailout.

But no consensus existed within the Democratic party, nor even among Democrats on the Agriculture committees. For example, Senate Agriculture Committee chairman Patrick J. Leahy, a Vermont Democrat, was at some odds with David L. Boren, a Democrat from Oklahoma and chairman of the Subcommittee on Credit. Much of their disagreement had to do with local interests, since Boren was from a district needing assistance, Leahy from a district giving it. "There's bound to be some difference of opinion between them," said Michael Dunne, an aide to Leahy.

Then again, some farm-state Democrats wanted to broaden the "institutional" aspects of the bailout to include aid that

would benefit farmers directly. Specifically, they wanted to include new forbearance requirements to stall foreclosures by the system and by the Farmers Home Administration. "Our concern is with the borrower, regardless of what lending system they're dealing with," said Timothy J. Penny, Democrat of Minnesota and a member of the House Agriculture Committee.

In addition, commercial banks and insurance groups took particular interest in the Farm Credit System rescue efforts because they believed previous bills gave the system an unfair advantage in the market for agricultural real estate loans. Their representatives vowed to fight any rescue package that did not keep their interests in mind. As a result, farm-state legislators were left with the seemingly impossible task of crafting a bill that encompassed the cross-cutting agendas of farm and banking groups, urban and rural members.

Farmers in the United States have always relied on credit to make ends meet. Farm borrowing increased five-fold between 1950 and 1980.

121

A Ready-Made Lobby

Beyond the "moral" imperative to preserve the system's ability to deliver credit, however, were two political forces putting added pressure on Congress to save the system: the farmer-borrower and the financial investor.

The cooperative nature of the system was its most meaningful characteristic, if for no other reason than it extended a many-tentacled reach into farm country. The system affected nearly every agricultural producer in the country and financed every type of agricultural product through loans for land, equipment, seed, and feed. Each of the local lending associations in the system was organized as a cooperative of farmer-borrowers. Each cooperative elected its own board of directors and formed a ready-made political network of farmers and ranchers who knew how to get in touch with representatives in Congress. "They're scattered through a majority of congressional districts," said Wayne Boutwell, director of the National Council for Farmer Cooperatives and a consultant on the system's congressional lobbying efforts. "When members go out to their districts it's hard to get away from them. They're everywhere."

Another political force with equal power came from Wall Street, where the system raised its cash. Urban members had a large stake in keeping the Farm Credit System on sound financial footing because its collapse would be felt in other financial markets. "Any time you weaken one part of the credit system, it has ramifications elsewhere," acknowledged Schumer.

The crucial link between system bonds and other investment instruments was the federal government. System bonds were technically backed only by the system's assets—that is, the loans to farmers and ultimately the land farmers used as collateral. But investors bought them on the widespread assumption that they were really guaranteed by the U.S. Treasury.

This implied federal guarantee gave the system a status on Wall Street that came close to matching that of a government agency. Its "agency status" allowed the system to sell bonds at much lower interest rates than bonds issued by private corporations. System bonds often sold at only a few tenths of an interest point above U.S. Treasury bills, considered the most secure paper in the world because it is backed by the full faith and credit of the federal government. Indeed, system bonds were viewed as highly reliable investments. They were purchased mainly by pension funds, banks, and other institutional investors looking for predictable, if relatively low, yields. (The bonds were considered so secure that federal law allowed commercial banks to use them instead of cash to meet part of their minimum reserve requirements.)

In mid-1987, the Farm Credit System had about $58 billion worth of bonds outstanding. It was generally believed that if a system bank were to declare bankruptcy and the federal government did not step in to guarantee the outstanding debt, the shock waves would be felt throughout the nation's money markets. Investor confidence in other agency status bonds, such as the Federal National Mortgage Association (Fannie Mae), would be seriously impaired. Some experts believed even U.S. bonds could be hurt, largely because a growing number of foreign investors were buying Treasury bills. Comparable farm credit agencies in Canada, Great Britain, and Japan are closely tied to their governments. "Those who hold our paper also hold Treasury paper," said Gene Swackhammer, president of the three Baltimore district Farm Credit System banks. "And foreign investors, in particular, do not seem to differentiate between implied and explicit guarantees."

Indeed, because most of these investor concerns were aired when the system first revealed its problems in 1985, Wall Street analysts said the market had already taken the situation into account and reacted accordingly when the system came back for help for the third time. The spread between rates on system bonds and Treasury issues rose sharply in 1985 but had since narrowed. "It's old news now," Richard Wilson, an analyst with the New York investment firm Merrill Lynch & Co. Inc., said in mid-1987, before either the House or Senate Agriculture Committee had begun writing a rescue bill. "I think most of the people in the Farm Credit System market are aware of the situation in Washington, and most feel that the system will be bailed out."

Agriculture Committee members who thought they could have a bill ready for floor action in the spring of 1987 still agreed with that assessment, but they were not yet ready to give the system a blank check. "It's like pouring money down a black hole," said Gene Moos, agriculture adviser to House majority leader Thomas S. Foley, a Washington Democrat who had served as chairman of the Agriculture Committee for many years.

Farmer Mac's Help

The ascension of "Farmer Mac" into the pantheon of government-sponsored secondary loan markets had been a foregone conclusion since the early spring of 1987. And as it turned out, creating a trading house for farm mortgages was a crucial part of new bailout legislation for the Farm Credit System. It was what the banking and insurance industries wanted in return for their pivotal support for the system's financial rescue.

"The banking lobby has commitments from 90 percent of the House to include some kind of secondary market," Representative de la Garza, chairman of the House Agriculture Committee, said as his committee began to craft its bill. "It has to be part of the package."

But what had seemed like a "done deal" suddenly looked a bit shaky when members of the House and Senate Agriculture committees finally sat down July 29 to mark up a system bailout bill. Key Democrats and Republicans began to wonder aloud what impact a secondary market would have on the system's ability to compete with private lenders for the most creditworthy borrowers. Their doubts were prompted by the system's estimates that private lenders could take advantage of the secondary market to win as much as 15 percent of the land loan market away from the quasi-federal system banks. "The question is whether the system can survive," said Oklahoma representative English.

Not coincidentally, members were worried about the system's ability to repay any federal loan that Congress might have to give it. "I'm being asked to put $6 billion into the Farm Credit System and [because of the secondary market] they're never going to be able to pay it back," griped Madigan.

Rural lawmakers were eager to come to the system's rescue, but commercial banking and insurance industry officials, still bitter about being left out of previous farm credit rescue legislation in 1985 and 1986, were afraid of letting their main competitors get the advantage. "If you're going to do something substantial for the Farm Credit System, equity would tend to dictate that you include something broader for commercial lenders," said Weldon Barton, a Washington lobbyist for the Independent Bankers Association of America, an organization of thousands of small banks, many of which compete directly with Farm Credit System banks. "Politically, the system is in a better situation working with us this time," he said.

Private lenders wanted a secondary market for farm real estate loans for one important reason: it would enable them to diversify their risk by pooling loans of varying geographic location and commodity type. They could also get their money back quickly by selling loans instead of waiting for payments to trickle in over years and years.

System officials, while privately opposed to the idea of a secondary market, essentially resigned themselves to the political necessity of including it in their request for federal assistance. "There's no question this is driven by political considerations," said John Waits, chief Washington lobbyist for the system.

The farm loan secondary market was to be patterned after three cousins that dominate the home loan business: Fannie Mae, Freddie Mac, and Ginnie Mae, nicknames for the Federal National Mortgage Association, the Federal Home Loan Mortgage Corporation, and the Government National Mortgage Association, respectively. Like many types of financial instruments—stocks, corporate bonds, and Treasury securities—home mortgages have their own highly developed secondary markets. In its simplest form, a secondary-market transaction occurs when a loan is sold by the original lender to someone else who will collect future payments on it. New secondary markets have sprung up for car loans, credit card debt, and manufacturers' notes receivable.

Fannie Mae and Freddie Mac are federally chartered, private organizations that were spun off from Ginnie Mae, a government-owned organization. The financial community perceives that securities sold through Fannie Mae and Freddie Mac are almost as good as if they were directly backed by the government. Thus they are said to have the vaunted "agency status," although such implicit guarantees have never been tested.

These markets have been credited with greatly expanding commercial lenders' ability to offer long-term, fixed-rate loans to homeowners, largely because agency status allowed these organizations to market securities at low interest rates. In 1986, mortgage-backed securities issued through the federally sponsored secondary markets totaled $260 billion, or about 70 percent of the $384 billion home loan market. Ten years ago those securities were 30 percent of the market.

A secondary market for agriculture, its proponents argued, would allow small agricultural banks and insurance companies to do the same for farm real estate loans. A study commissioned by the American Council of Life Insurance concluded that a secondary market could reduce interest rates by up to 1 percentage point and ultimately shore up farmland values by $27.5 billion. Of the $8 billion in new loans each year created in the agricultural sector, about $500 million to $2 billion would go in the secondary market, the study concluded.

Yet pressure for a secondary market for farm loans raised an obvious question: Why were commercial lenders so anxious to get in the unpredictable business of making farm loans?

"A lot of major insurance companies have their roots in agriculture," said Leslie G. Horsager, vice president of the Prudential Agricultural Group in Newark, N.J. "There's a tremendous amount of loyalty in the senior management of these companies toward agriculture. You don't walk away from that kind of business quickly."

But banking and insurance industry officials were not so anxious to start such a market on their own. They insisted that the only way to avoid the expensive start-up costs and image-building problems of a new secondary market was to give it federal sponsorship, or agency status. They proposed to make it a corporation of the Farm Credit System, which already had a federal imprimatur.

Administration officials and some members of Congress, however, said that creating a secondary market within the system would force the federal government, ultimately, to guarantee commercial lenders' securities. "I regard the bankers' [proposal] as a rape of taxpayers and farmers for the benefit of bankers," Madigan said. "They're asking Congress to give them permission to steal away the best borrowers from the system, but they get a government guarantee."

"It's an interesting political tradeoff, if that's what it is," said Treasury's Sethness. "In order to get the support of banks and insurance companies, the Farm Credit System has put a gun to its head and is ready to pull the trigger."

A Novel Solution

As expected, the secondary market provision proved to be the sluice for quick and widespread approval of the bailout measure among urban and rural lawmakers alike. Provisions requiring the system and the Farmers Home Administration to establish a broad range of "borrowers' rights" and forebearance policies also smoothed the way with populist-oriented Democrats. The ultimate success of the bill, however, came back to the original question—how to pay for the system's multibillion dollar bailout request.

The Senate Agriculture Committee, for its part, came up with the final icebreaker. It divised a complicated and multilayered funding mechanism that would allow a federal assistance board, appointed to oversee the system, through yet another federal assistance "corporation," to issue up to $4 billion in fifteen-year bonds on the system's behalf. The government would pay all the interest on the bonds for the first five years, and half the interest for the next five years, leaving the remaining five-year obligation up to the system itself. Committee members maintained that would limit the actual cost to the government to about $200 million a year, or a total of about $1.5 billion over ten years.

A crucial budgetary obstacle to this clever scheme was cleared when the White House Office of Management and Budget, after lengthy negotiations with Senate Agriculture leaders, determined that the assistance corporation would not be a government entity but would be treated instead as a government-sponsored enterprise. This small but important distinction placed the assistance corporation in the same quasi-private category as the system itself. As a result, bonds issued by the assistance corporation to bail out system banks would not be considered federal borrowing, and the distribution of the $4 billion would not be considered government outlays, even though they were to carry an explicit guarantee of eventual repayment by the Treasury.

The Congressional Budget Office (CBO), the nonpartisan fiscal analyst for Congress, said the budgetary treatment agreed to by White House budget officials was a "very close call." "The private nature of the corporation is questionable," the CBO report stated, because it "would be created by the federal government to carry out a perceived governmental responsibility.... Its activities would be controlled by the federal government, and the financial risk associated with its activities would be borne almost entirely by the government."

If the assistance corporation had been treated as a governmental entity, CBO said, the real cost of the bailout to the government would have been about $1.3 billion in fiscal 1988 alone and would total $3.5 billion through fiscal 1992.

The novel funding idea did not escape the notice of other members of Congress. In early 1987, barely two months into the new congressional session, Senate Budget Committee chairman Lawton Chiles of Florida complained of at least five new proposals to set up federally chartered corporations to perform activities that ordinarily would be funded by Congress directly. Treasury secretary James A. Baker III shared Chiles's concern about the trend. "We really don't believe that these off-budget government sponsored enterprises are particularly useful," Baker said. "We know they're not presenting an accurate picture of the government's true liabilities or contigent liabilities, and quite often they are used to hide governmental subsidies under a private sector label."

A Future Together

In the end, the system had to pay a steep political price for its continued existence. In return for federal aid, Congress required system officials to put into motion the most extensive overhaul of the thirty-seven-bank lending network since the 1930s. The Federal Intermediate Credit Banks in each of the system's twelve districts were forced to merge with their sister Federal Land Banks within six months. This was the gist of the system's own reorganization proposal—developed under intense congressional pressure—which would eventually allow farmer-borrowers who held controlling shares in the system to vote on whether to merge the districts themselves. The system could end up with as few as six districts, although the general decision-making powers would remain with farmer-borrowers at the local association level.

But for at least fifteen years, or as long as it takes the system to pay off its new federal debt, the real decisions about loan rates and new bond issues and foreclosures and lending policy will be made by the three-member assistance board, which will include the secretaries of agriculture and the Treasury, assigned to oversee the use of the rescue money. In other words, the Farm Credit System will be under the effective control and responsibility of the federal government. The bonds used to bolster the finances of ailing system banks will be guaranteed, for all practical purposes, by the federal government. The stock that farmer-borrowers purchased as a condition for getting loans will also be guaranteed at full value for five years. Borrowers who are threatened by default will enjoy new federal protections against foreclosure and assurances of government-sponsored mediation.

In the meantime, the Farmers Home Administration stopped foreclosure proceedings against thousands of delinquent borrowers and announced in early 1988 that it would be offering to refinance about $9 billion worth of nonpaying loans at newly subsidized interest rates. Private lenders, too, will be gearing up to offer fixed-rate, low-interest land loans with the help of a new secondary market bolstered by $1.5 billion in federal backing. The Treasury has been required to underwrite (lend) that much to the secondary market to cover excessive loan losses.

As the congressman said, soon the government will be backing every farm loan in the country.

Chapter 7

Payment-in-Kind

Money may not grow on trees, but since the spring of 1986, something a whole lot like it has been sprouting in grain bins.

In March of that year the Reagan administration quietly instituted a program that changed the face of U.S. agriculture. On the orders of Secretary John R. Block, the Agriculture Department began the process of issuing certificates to farmers as partial "payment-in-kind" for their federal crop subsidies. Farmers who normally received price- and income-support payments in cash could opt to take much of their benefits in an equivalent dollar amount of in-kind certificates. These so-called PIKs could then be redeemed for the government's massive stocks of wheat, feed grains, rice, or milk, which farmers could use themselves for feed or sell on the open market as they saw fit. If nothing else, it was thought, farmers would get an equal return on the commodities and the government would be able to unload some of its burdensome surpluses.

At first, the new PIK program seemed like no big deal. Congress in past years had authorized the agriculture secretary to use government commodities as payments-in-kind to farmers, and the department had tried a number of variations on the idea with varying degrees of success. A 1983-1984 payment-in-kind program proved to be expensive and had other negative side effects, but otherwise these schemes had no lasting implications for basic U.S. farm policy.

As the new PIK certificates began to circulate through farm country, however, something strange and unusual began to happen. Many PIK recipients found that selling the certificates themselves brought a higher cash return than selling the underlying commodities. Farmers, grain merchants, and market speculators appeared eager to pay high premiums for the grain-backed paper, offering in some parts of the country as much as 15 to 25 percent more than the face value of the certificates. In other words, a farmer who received a certificate redeemable for $10,000 worth of government-owned grain could sell the paper to a neighbor for $11,500, who in turn could sell it for $12,000 to the local grain elevator operator, who might be able to fetch $12,500 from one of the big grain merchants, such as Cargill Inc.

Payment-in-kind (PIK) certificates are redeemed for the government's surplus stock of wheat, feed grains, rice, or milk, which farmers may use for feed or sell on the open market. However, many PIK recipients found that selling the certificates brought a higher cash return than selling the underlying commodities.

or Harvest States Cooperatives.

The premiums were spurred by a variety of economic factors converging on the Farm Belt—mainly the tight supply of storage space throughout the Midwest and the concurrent need to put an impending bumper harvest into bins. But for sellers and buyers alike, the grain-backed paper created a whole new set of marketing opportunities. "You start a new farm program, and there's going to be some guys who figure out how to make money from it," said country elevator operator Dave Hanson, who runs a storage plant in Valley City, N.D.

And as only seems to happen in the convoluted logic of agricultural economics, the PIK certificates took on the characteristics of a new kind of money—only this legal tender was backed by wheat, barley, and corn instead of gold or silver. It could be bought, sold, and traded like any other marketable security. Rather sophisticated market networks soon evolved to move the paper all over the country. A lot of people—farm-state politicians among them—thought it was better than cash. "During the next four or five years," warned Sen. Pete V. Domenici, "we are about to create a new kind of currency in the United States."

Sen. Pete V. Domenici, R-N.M., warned that PIK certificates would soon represent "a new kind of currency in the United States."

Indeed, in less than two years, more than $13 billion worth of this grain-backed paper was circulated through the agricultural heartland, compliments of the Reagan administration and a more than acquiescent Congress. Another $5 billion was expected to come off Agriculture Department printing presses in early 1988, and that much and more will no doubt be on its way from Washington, D.C., in subsequent years as the Agriculture Department tries to pump up the market, get rid of some more surpluses, and—most importantly—keep a firm federal grip on the farm economy. (See Table 7-1.)

At the Secretary's Discretion

Oddly enough, Congress will have had little to do with this brainstorm of agricultural policy making. Most members had no idea what would happen to the PIK certificates when they gave the administration authority to issue them. They were merely following a long political tradition of ceding broad discretionary authority to the executive branch to carry out federal farm programs. The PIK program is just one—and, as it turned out, the most important—example of how much power the agricul-

Table 7-1   Payment-in-Kind Certificate Issuances, May 1986 to March 1988

	Program	Value of certificates
Fiscal year 1986		
May	1986 crop deficiency payments	$ 1,009,000,000
	1986 crop diversion payments	342,000,000
	Ethanol subsidies	25,000,000
	Export subsidies	26,000,000
	Miscellaneous farm programs	1,000,000
August	1986 crop deficiency payments	1,004,000,000
Total (Fiscal year 1986)		$ 2,407,000,000
Fiscal year 1987		
October	1986 crop deficiency payments	$ 223,000,000
	Conservation reserve program	83,000,000
	Emergency feed program	85,000,000
	Ethanol subsidies	29,000,000
	Export subsidies	710,000,000
	Miscellaneous farm programs	17,000,000
December	1986 crop deficiency payments	1,127,000,000
	1987 crop deficiency payments	2,650,000,000
	1987 crop diversion payments	1,184,000,000
February	Disaster payments	386,000,000
	1986 crop deficiency payments	15,000,000
March	1986 crop deficiency payments	390,000,000
May	Conservation reserve program	327,000,000
July	1986 crop deficiency payments	63,000,000
August	Disaster payments	170,000,000
Total (Fiscal year 1987)		$ 7,459,000,000
Fiscal year 1988		
October	1986 crop deficiency payments	$ 1,468,000,000
	Conservation reserve program	778,000,000
December	1987 crop deficiency payments	1,337,000,000
February [a]	1987 crop deficiency payments	1,178,000,000
March [a]	1987 crop deficiency payments	1,436,000,000
May [a]	1988 crop deficiency payments	2,150,000,000
	1988 crop diversion payments	724,000,000
Total (Fiscal year 1988)		$ 9,071,000,000
Total (Fiscal years 1986-1988) [a]		$ 18,937,000,000

Source: U.S. Department of Agriculture, Economic Research Service.

Note: Month indicates when program funds first became available.

[a] Announced as of March 31, 1988.

134

ture secretary has to shape and control farm policy. In the 1985 farm bill, for instance, Congress actually gave the secretary authority to implement virtually any farm policy, from mandatory production controls to marketing loans. This discretionary power is so vast that the next president could completely rewrite U.S. farm policy the moment a new agriculture secretary is appointed in 1989. The new secretary would not have to seek approval from Congress until late 1990, the year existing farm law officially expires.

Since the 1988 presidential candidates expressed a wide range of farm policy predilections, such a scenario was not out of the question. A Democrat such as Richard A. Gephardt of Missouri, if he were elected president, could immediately order a nationwide referendum of farmers to determine if they would prefer to operate under strict production controls as established by the government. Gephardt was the House sponsor of a proposed bill requiring the secretary to do just that, but a provision in the 1985 farm bill already would allow an agriculture secretary more sympathetic to a mandatory controls policy to put the issue to a vote of farmers. On the other hand, Republican Robert Dole of Kansas, if he were elected president, could order the implementation of a marketing loan for corn and soybeans to allow farmers to sell their crops at rock-bottom prices and still get a guaranteed price from the government. It was a policy he could never get President Reagan or the rest of Congress to approve while he was the Republican leader of the Senate. Yet the 1985 farm bill contains a marketing loan provision, to be implemented at the agriculture secretary's discretion.

Of course, Congress does not give the administration such wide latitude in the conduct of farm programs just to avoid its own responsibility to set policy. Farm law is crafted through a sophisticated political process involving detailed negotiations between the Agriculture committees, the secretary of agriculture, and, to a growing degree, the White House Office of Management and Budget (OMB). Conflicting policies are often written into law with the unstated but clear understanding among farm-state lawmakers that the agriculture secretary will consult with them before making any abrupt changes.

Even under the confines of these political understandings, however, the agriculture secretary maintains almost autocratic control over many important details of farm policy. The 1985 farm bill gives the secretary much discretion in setting price-support rates for wheat and feed grains. The secretary also determines, for the most part, the acreage reduction requirements for farmers who participate in federal farm programs.

The Presses Roll

The new PIK program became the ultimate example of how far the secretary's discretionary powers could reach. Many experts believe Block and his successor, Richard E. Lyng, have taken the new PIK certificate program to the point where it now forms the underpinning of a new U.S. farm policy. And, in many respects, PIKs *are* the farm bill of 1985.

The certificates are used mainly in the government's most expensive benefit program—deficiency payments, income supports covering the difference between the price farmers get for their crops and a higher target price set by Congress. In 1985 Congress required the Agriculture Department to make a portion of the anticipated deficiency payments available to farmers at the beginning of the year, instead of after harvest. Most of these payments could be made with in-kind certificates.

Lyng at first made 40 percent of the deficiency payments in advance, leading to an issue of $1.2 billion worth of certificates in April 1986. Another $300 million were issued in connection with separate cotton benefits and other export programs. In early May the secretary announced a new program to subsidize the purchase of grain by ethanol producers, paying producers generic certificates worth one bushel for every 2.5 bushels they purchased from private stocks. Certificates also became the currency of choice for the Export Enhancement Program, a $2 billion effort to encourage exporters to ship grain overseas at lower, more competitive prices, and for the Targeted Export Assistance Program, which funded export promotion activities for a variety of agricultural products.

Then in August 1986, in response to a summerlong drought in the Southeast, Lyng announced he would increase the advance deficiency payments by another 10 percent, to be paid entirely with in-kind certificates. That led to a second issue of about $1 billion worth of certificates, which was followed by another $550 million worth in special disaster-relief benefits for drought and flood-stricken farmers. Finally, PIKs were issued in lieu of cash in connection with a new Conservation Reserve Program, which paid farmers to take erodible land out of production for ten years, at a cost of more than $1 billion a year.

Even so, farmers and agriculture industry leaders were pressing for more. "The premium you see on certificates is an indication that people don't feel there are enough," Timothy J. Engel, a wheat merchandiser for Harvest States Cooperatives in St. Paul, Minn., said in early 1987. Engel said the amount of certificates in circulation could double without seriously affecting their market value.

Indeed, some of the more avid proponents of the new PIK program credited it with pumping new life into a moribund rural economy. The bullish market for certificates spawned a whole network of services related to their circulation. New brokerage firms were established to handle certificate transactions, and some even began to trade the paper on a "forward contract" basis, creating a separate futures market for certificates. Country grain elevator operators and grain merchants also cashed in on the action by acting as brokers, buying and selling the certificates daily, much like market-sensitive securities or options. "We try to buy them every day, no matter what the market is," Hanson said.

Richard E. Lyng succeeded John R. Block as President Reagan's agriculture secretary.

Without a doubt, the new PIK plan has been the most popular farm program invented since the government came up with the idea of subsidizing farmers for what they could not make on their own. Of course, government policy makers seized on the phenomenon by speeding up the printing presses. The Agriculture Department pulled out the stops, to the extent that by 1988 nearly a third of all farm subsidies were being paid out in certificates instead of cash. The scrip was ubiquitous in the months leading up to the November 1986 elections, when control of the Senate hinged on races in key farm states, and, if possible, it was even more prevalent in the presidential election year of 1988.

By the time the 1986 elections were over, the perceived political benefits of the new currency overcame all other policy and budgetary concerns. The paper was so pervasive—so wedded to both the farm economy and congressional spending habits—that no one in government dared mention the possibility of taking it away. "We feel the concept has been working and has been a success," Ralph Klopfenstein, administrator of the program for the Agriculture Department, said in mid-1986. "All of the reading I have within the department is, we want to expand it."

For farm-state politicians, the certificates represented a relatively unrestricted funding pipeline to their main constituency. The peculiar structure of the federal price-support program made in-kind payments exempt from the antideficit spending restrictions of Gramm-Rudman-Hollings, a law that otherwise forced across-the-board cutbacks on all cash subsidies to farmers. Since PIK payments did not involve direct cash outlays, they were not subject to reduction under Gramm-Rudman. When cash payments were reduced 4.3 percent under the 1986 Gramm-Rudman cutbacks, the 40-percent advance payment farmers got in PIKs were not reduced unless the holder later decided to redeem them for cash instead of commodities. In addition, the market offered the farmer a premium of up to 25 percent on the certificate. "The choice of PIK against cash payments thus has an immediate effect on producer incomes," said Joseph V. Kennedy, former budget analyst for the White House Office of Management and Budget and an expert on the PIK program. In plain political terms, the exemption from Gramm-Rudman meant that PIK certificates were the only largess farm-state members of Congress or the administration could make free use of in a tight budgetary environment.

New Wrinkle to Old Scheme

The seeds of this money-making bonanza were planted in the 1985 farm bill. During that year's House and Senate agricultural debates, which revolved around the soaring cost of farm programs, the Agriculture committees included provisions for making in-kind payments to farmers who qualify for certain federal benefits. The scheme was first propounded with the idea that it would cost less than giving farmers hard cash. The government had already bought and paid for the grain, it was argued, so giving farmers a deed to the commodities, which they could then sell on the open market, would be an economical way to maintain a high level of federal benefits.

The government had tried a similar scheme in 1983, when the Reagan administration offered government-owned grain to farmers who agreed to take their land out of production for a year. The 1983 PIK program required farmers to take physical possession of the grain, which in many cases was stored far away from the farmers who wanted to claim it. The program turned into a logistical nightmare that no one in the Agriculture Department or Congress cared to relive. So when the new farm bill became law in December 1985, department officials came up with a new wrinkle on the old PIK game. They decided to give farmers dollar-denominated certificates instead of direct title to the grain itself. That way a farmer who did not have access to government-stored grain could simply sell the certificate to someone who did.

Daniel G. Amstutz, who was under secretary of agriculture for commodity programs, also decided to make the certificates generic—that is, redeemable for any commodity stored in government grain bins. That meant a wheat farmer could exchange a certificate for corn, other feed grains, rice, cotton, or milk products. More importantly, it gave the certificates characteristics of a true currency, able to flow to any region of the country as demand dictated.

The premium prices for PIK certificates were spurred largely by the short supply of storage space throughout most of the Midwest and the concurrent need to put impending harvests into bins. The shortage made a PIK certificate all the more valuable because it could be redeemed for storage space as well as the surplus grain that occupied it. "The certificates represent real, concrete things, and one of those things is storage space," said Katharina Zimmer, a grains analyst for the Merrill Lynch brokerage firm in New York. "If you know you'll need storage space a month down the road, you hoard the stuff."

Since certificates ultimately could be redeemed only for government-controlled commodities, the way the Agriculture Department priced those commodities had considerable influence over the value of the certificates as well as with the market prices of commodities in general. The certificates took on even more value when the Agriculture Department, in another unilateral decision that had major policy implications, began releasing government-controlled grain from storage bins at below book value.

The grain controlled by the government must by law remain in storage until it brings a price at least equal to what the government paid for it. The only other way for the department to dispose of its surplus is through export donation programs, such as the PL 480 Food for Peace program, or through other food giveaway programs specifically authorized by Congress, such as cheese and butter distributions to the poor. The new PIK certificates, as it turned out, were another way to unload

PIK certificates could be redeemed for cash or old grain, or they could buy precious storage space for incoming crops.

government-controlled grain that could not find a market at the original payment prices. By making bargain-basement grain available only to PIK certificate-holders, who could then sell the grain at a profit, the department effectively took control of the entire market, since it was the department that would daily establish the all-important release prices.

Yet in choosing this method of setting release prices for government-controlled grain, the department "denied itself even greater flexibility in ... managing its large inventory of commodities," Kennedy argued in *Choices*, the journal of the American Agricultural Economics Association. "Whether the department should exercise the type of micromanagement ... has never been discussed at a high level within the administration. Certainly it has not been publicly debated."

A Bear Market

Ultimately, the PIK certificates had a negative, or bearish, effect on grain prices by bringing surplus stocks onto the open market. What the government had been buying up to keep farm prices high was now being released onto the open market. As more grain came onto the market, prices went down, creating a self-perpetuating condition of farmers being forced to sell their new harvests to the government because they could not get a price that bettered the federal support rate. As a result, farmers ended up relying even more on federal benefits, not less. In a word, the government's marketing strategy for surplus grain was: buy high and sell low.

The Agriculture Department added another feature to the PIK certificate program that only spurred farmers' interest and involvement in the program. As farmers put their new crops "under loan"—that is, put their crops into storage in return for a federal price-support loan—the department would allow them to redeem the same crops with PIK certificates. Farmers could redeem their loan crops immediately, and what is more, they could do so at a lower price than the loan rate. In other words, the government would buy a farmer's wheat crop at one price, then turn around and sell the same crop back to the farmer at a lower price—so long as the farmer paid for it in PIK certificates. The resale price was determined by the Agriculture Department on a daily, county-by-county basis.

In effect, this paper shuffle—it quickly became known in farm country as "quick PIK"—forgave that portion of the price-support loan that a farmer could not repay if the crop were sold on the open market. A federal loan issued to a corn farmer at the 1986 rate of $1.92 a bushel could be "paid off" in one Iowa county at the rate of $1.20 a bushel. The farmer would then sell the corn at $1.20 or better and keep the seventy-two-cent difference paid by the government.

Ironically, the same principle was contained in the "marketing loan" system of price supports that was favored by many farm-state legislators but that, in the case of wheat and feed grains, was consistently rejected by the Reagan administration. Under the marketing loan policy, farmers must repay only as much of their loans as their crops bring on the market. Any shortfall would be forgiven. Congress in 1985 required the agriculture secretary to offer marketing loans to cotton and rice farmers but made the program discretionary for wheat and feed grains. The Reagan administration steadfastly opposed making official use of the marketing loan for wheat, corn, and soybeans, mainly because of complaints from the president's budget advisers that it would cost too much, and from his national security advisers that the policy would push prices down so low as to harm grain-producing foreign allies that depended heavily on grain sales.

The Agriculture Department effectively found a way around those political problems. Block and Lyng put a de facto marketing loan into effect through the PIK certificate program, thereby masking the real cost of the program and protecting it from any negative international implications.

The Hidden Costs

The sudden emergence of PIK certificates as a federal spending device presented a host of unresolved questions for policy makers and budget writers. Though the Agriculture Department had some control over the flow of certificates onto the market, the subsequent transactions were unregulated and vulnerable to various methods of market manipulation. That posed farm-state legislators with yet another paradox in an agriculture policy that continued to make no dent in the nation's massive stockpiles. "If it weren't for the certificates, corn prices would be 15 cents a bushel higher," said Zimmer of Merrill Lynch. "The lower the price of corn, the more bushels you can redeem with certificates. The thing feeds on itself."

And even as the known expenditures for farm programs spiraled to record heights, the hidden costs of this new wrinkle in agriculture budgeting was confounding efforts to bring the federal deficit under control. PIK certificates added to the deficit in one obvious way by releasing government-owned grain stocks at lower prices than the government paid for them, creating an immediate shortfall that ultimately had to be made up by the taxpayer.

The government takes control of surplus grain when a farmer, in exchange for a price-support loan, agrees to keep a crop off the market for a limited time. This is done to prevent all crops from being dumped on the open market at harvest. When a farmer puts a crop under loan, the crop becomes collateral. If a better price than the loan rate is not available in the marketplace, the farmer may default on the loan, forfeit the grain to the government, and keep the original loan money. This default scenario has been a recurrent condition since 1981 because Congress kept the loan rate well above prevailing world market prices. Even in 1986, after Congress allowed loan rates for wheat and feed grains to drop by more than 25 percent, market prices for the most part remained below the loan rates.

The new PIK certificates, as it turned out, were another way to dispose of government-controlled grain that could not find a market at the loan-inflated price. The Agriculture Department accomplished this by setting a redemption price for its grain that is pegged to "prevailing" market prices in each county. In the case of wheat, the average rate was $2.38 a bushel in 1986. But most of the grain owned by the government was "purchased" from farmers who defaulted on their crop loans in previous years at a rate of $3.30 a bushel.

Rough calculations showed that this ninety-two-cents-a-bushel shortfall resulted in an immediate $86.1 million loss to the government's inventory of wheat when PIK certificates were first issued in May 1986. As of August 27, four months after the program began, the government had assumed losses of $350 million on its total stocks of wheat, corn, grain sorghum, rye,

In the mid-1980s corn had to be piled on the ground when grain storage elevators became full.

oats, barley, soybeans, and rice. By the end of the year the loss was more than $1 billion.

Agriculture Department officials argued that the Commodity Credit Corporation (CCC), the federal agency that distributes price and income-support payments to farmers and stores their crops, would have incurred large losses even without the PIK certificate program. The CCC had to pay commercial warehouses an average of thirty-six cents a bushel a year to store grain that could not be disposed of. For wheat and corn, that amounted to more than $1 billion a year.

But congressional budget officials, already frustrated by their inability to get a handle on CCC expenditures, found they were further handcuffed by the imponderable task of trying to project the cost of any farm spending proposal that used PIK certificates in lieu of cash. The problem stemmed from the way the CCC is structured. The CCC is a "corporation" of the government that operates on a revolving fund, borrowing one year from Treasury and paying it back the next. Congress reimburses the CCC for its annual losses, which occur as a result of direct subsidies and loan losses.

A portion of those net losses shows up when the CCC sells grain for less than it paid for it. But the bearish effect of dumping CCC grain onto the marketplace has an additional impact on the budget. The depressed prices for market grain lead to an even wider disparity between actual prices and the higher target price that Congress uses to determine farm subsidy rates. The CCC ends up paying bigger income subsidies, which Congress must then repay the following year. Judging how much PIK certificates are influencing market prices, however, is nearly impossible to predict. "What we're seeing is a circular thing," said G. William Hoagland, Republican staff director of the Senate Budget Committee. "We've paid for these commodities once. The purpose is to take them out of the market to relieve the pressure on prices. Now we're putting those commodities back into the market. It's like chasing your tail."

A study by the General Accounting Office (GAO) estimated the PIK program had added $100 million to $650 million to total CCC outlays in fiscal 1986, although the GAO noted that the cost was at least partially offset by an estimated storage savings of $170 million to $250 million. The study was also careful to say that different market conditions could produce either larger costs or savings.

The Office of Management and Budget, though less supportive of the program than its advocates in the Agriculture Department, apparently decided PIKs were worth the extra 5 to 10 percent they cost to the government. "I have to confess we don't fully understand it," Ron Landis, head of OMB's agriculture division, told a convention of grain dealers in March 1987. "I don't know if it will ever be possible to put a price tag on the impact of PIK certificates. At OMB we do not have a policy position on expanding or contracting PIKS. We do have a concern, founded on less than total understanding, that there not be so large a quantity issued that it creates a substantial adverse impact on the market. But we don't know what that 'too much' is.

"In the short term," he continued, "we need access to those stocks and I think PIK certificates do a good job of that."

In the meantime, the new PIK program was drawing nothing but rave reviews throughout the agriculture community. The Grand Forks (N.D.) *Herald* newspaper discovered that one of its most popular features was a daily survey of elevator operators for the going rates for PIK certificates. The University of Nebraska's "AgNet" computer database listed offers to buy and sell PIK certificates along with traditional ads for feed and storage. Corn farmers in Iowa, where storage space was particularly tight, reported some transactions as high as 125 percent of par, or face value.

No small measure of the PIK success was that the new market was fun to play. "We've even created a whole new vocabulary for it," said Ruth Pederson, wife of a Northwood, N.D., farmer. "When you redeem a certificate, we say you're going to 'PIK it out.'" Wayne Angell, a governor of the Federal Reserve Board and a Kansas farmer, began an interview with his own question: "What are they going for now?" Told the rates were heading upwards toward 125 percent, he deadpanned: "I'm apparently not very smart. I sold mine for only 107 percent."

No Oversight

PIK certificates are as good as gold to many farmers and grain traders, but unlike most securities traded in the United States, they are virtually unregulated by the government. Angell

Wayne Angell, a Kansas farmer, served as a governor of the Federal Reserve Board.

145

believed regulation would come if and when the market players themselves desired it. Otherwise, he said, there is little need for intervention. "The U.S. government bond market is largely unregulated, and it is the most efficient market that I've ever seen," Angell said.

A spokesperson for the Commodity Futures Trading Commission (CFTC), which oversees trading on commodities, said the CFTC has no role in regulating PIK certificates because they involve "actual delivery" of a commodity. Officials at the Securities and Exchange Commission (SEC) knew little about the PIK program even after it had been in operation for nearly a year. They said the certificates seemed more like a warehouse receipt than an actual security. An official in the market regulation division said the SEC might have jurisdiction if a formal complaint were made of fraud in sales.

The Agriculture Department is thus the only regulator of the PIK program, and its oversight duties mainly involve taking strict precautions to make sure the certificates cannot be counterfeited. Because PIK certificates play directly on the price of grain, however, some experts worry that they are as vulnerable to arbitrage and other forms of price manipulation as any futures contract.

The Agriculture Department has autocratic control in setting the prices at which CCC stocks can be released in each county. That information, along with the number of certificates the department decides to issue at any one time, is quickly becoming the determinate factor of grain prices overall. "The pricing of certificates is the only game in town," said John Gordley, a former aide to Kansas senator Dole and one of the instigators of the certificate program. "I did foresee them becoming like a currency. Never did I anticipate the amount of power it would put in the department's hands. All of the export houses are now hoarding these things. They're playing an arbitrage game with respect to how the Agriculture Department is pegging the release levels on stocks.

"A lot of money is being gained and lost playing the float," he said.

Many policy analysts who see advantages in the PIK program nonetheless were critical of the way it was put into law, and then implemented. "The administration did not have a clear understanding of the new certificate program when it first approved the used of certificates in lieu of cash in early 1986,"

Kennedy wrote. "Policy officials were exhausted by the long process required to complete the 1985 farm bill.... Since certificates were only a small, albeit significant, aspect of the commodity programs, certificates received only a small proportion of attention." Kennedy added: "We failed to see the impact certificates would have on the way farmers used the loan program."

Other observers, however, believe key policy makers in the administration were fully aware of the potential for PIK certificates during the 1985 farm bill debate. Chuck Lambert, an assistant professor at Central State Missouri University, noted in response to Kennedy's paper that the Reagan administration had put a completely new emphasis on farm programs, away from price stabilization and increased farm incomes, and toward stocks management, international competition, and lower federal expenditures. The PIK program, he said, helped the administration accomplish those goals, mainly because Congress had given Block and Lyng such wide latitude in their discretionary powers.

The final irony, of course, is that an administration otherwise devoted to deregulation and a free market philosophy enthusiastically adopted PIK certificates as a way to increase its manipulation of the agricultural marketplace.

Chapter 8

Agricultural Trade

Over the first seven years of his administration, President Reagan tried hard to sell his free-market farm policy to a highly skeptical Congress. Having failed at that, he spent his remaining months in office asking the rest of the world to buy it instead.

In his own quixotic way, Reagan was trying to achieve on a global scale what he could not get Congress even to consider at home: the complete elimination of farm subsidies by the year 2000. When he introduced that notion to U.S. trading partners in July 1987, it was the most radical idea ever presented on agriculture. No one before had ever dared to challenge such a fundamental precept of the industrial world. What is more, the administration wanted a positive answer before the end of 1988.

Yet outside Reagan's inner circle of advisers, no one really believed the lame-duck administration would get more than a French shrug from foreign politicians, who, if anything, put even more importance on protecting farmers from financial uncertainty than the farmer-doting U.S. Congress. Many European leaders believed the administration was merely grandstanding. "It's impossible, it's unrealistic, to say that in the future there will be no support for agriculture," complained Jacques Vonthron, a Washington delegate of the European Commission (EC), the administrative arm of the twelve-nation European Economic Community. "The main reason it was proposed was for shock value."

Since 1981, when Reagan came to the White House, Congress had summarily rejected such sweeping proposals from the president in two major farm bills and repeated budget requests.

Farm-state lawmakers in both parties were not about to do away with popular U.S. price-support programs, which sent a record $26 billion into farm country in 1986 and were expected to deliver an average of $17 billion to $20 billion a year to farmers at least through 1991. "The administration still wants to phase out price supports, but they lost all momentum for it in Congress," said Fred Sanderson, a senior fellow at the National Center for Food and Agricultural Policy, Resources for the Future, a Washington think tank. "And there is the ugly fact that, on both sides of the Atlantic, governments have been rebuffed in trying to make only slight reductions in farm subsidies."

Clayton Yeutter served as U.S. trade representative during the Reagan administration and helped formulate the radical U.S. proposal to end all world agricultural subsidies.

Given this political reality on Capitol Hill, Reagan's advisers, led by Agriculture Secretary Richard E. Lyng and U.S. Trade Representative Clayton Yeutter, proposed in mid-1987 to shift the administration's focus away from Washington and onto a new round of international trade talks that were getting under way in Geneva, Switzerland. They persuaded the president that the only chance of getting his farm policies enacted into law was to convince U.S. competitors in the rest of the world to follow suit. Reagan conceded as much when he introduced his ambitious plan for global cutbacks in farm subsidies. "No nation can unilaterally abandon current policies without being devastated by the policies of other countries," he said. "The only hope is for a major international agreement that commits everyone to the same actions and timetable."

Indeed, in a significant breakthrough that actually preceded announcement of the U.S. proposal, major exporting nations in late 1986 agreed to discuss agricultural subsidies at high-level trade talks, held under the auspices of the General Agreement on Tariffs and Trade (GATT). This ninety-five-member organization works like a United Nations of trade; a GATT agreement to eliminate or reduce agricultural subsidies would have the power of an international treaty. Since 1948 GATT has been the main venue and vehicle for instigating and enforcing world trade pacts.

Of course, getting U.S. trading partners to discuss the plan does not advance it very far, and members of Congress, in responding to the Reagan proposal, were still skeptical of the administration's tack. Senate Agriculture chairman Patrick J. Leahy called the proposal "unrealistic and unachievable," while House Agriculture chairman E. "Kika" de la Garza termed it a

150

"maximum expectation" that ultimately was an "unrealistic stance." But administration officials took heart in the fact that neither man dismissed the concept out of hand, and that farm-state members in general were reticent about the proposal. One senior House Agriculture member, Democrat Charles W. Stenholm of Texas, applauded Lyng and Yeutter for abandoning the idea of ending subsidies unilaterally and moving instead toward a multilateral approach. "They've begun to live in the world as it is," Stenholm said.

In fact, by 1988, U.S. officials and many agricultural trade experts had come to believe the time was right for a worldwide reappraisal of governmental intervention policies. Not since World War II had so many governments been considering major changes. Changing conditions in agricultural technology, in various countries' farm economies, and in their global trade relationships were spawning new doubts—even in the most entrenched of rural societies—that farm programs should be immune from change. Impending national elections in France and West Germany (and the United States) were seen as new opportunities for getting quick results. "The Europeans have to posture like crazy for negotiating position, but they come up to you individually and they say, 'These things have to change,'" said one official at the World Bank in Washington. "You would not have seen that three years ago."

That is because foreign leaders now seemed to recognize that governmental farm subsidies were hurting, instead of helping, the world agricultural economy. There was a growing consensus that in seeking to shield farmers from the vagaries of weather and economic forces, governments had actually distorted farm prices and land values, created artificially high food prices, and—most importantly—begun a wholesale raid on national treasuries. Indeed, there seemed to be one overriding reason governments besides the United States were willing to negotiate new rules for agricultural trade: farm subsidies cost too much.

Rep. Charles W. Stenholm, D-Texas, applauded Reagan administration officials who called for abandoning the idea of ending farm subsidies unilaterally and moving instead toward a multilateral approach.

Budget Pressures

The United States may have spent $26 billion in 1986 on its farm price-support subsidies, plus another $14 billion on other agricultural programs, but the Europeans were spending as much, if not more. The cost of the European Community's

Common Agricultural Policy (CAP), to which all member countries must contribute, soared to $26 billion in 1987, up from $8 billion only ten years earlier. Expenses could go even higher if surpluses increased or world prices continued to decline, officials said.

Pressure had been building within the European Community to cut agricultural expenses. Britain had begun sounding more like the United States on budget issues, arguing for sharp cutbacks in subsidies; new Latin members Spain and Portugal were pressing for more rural development funds, a different kind of help than the community was used to providing for agriculture. Even France, once the most agriculturally protective government in Europe, was moving away from its hardline position on the CAP. (Not coincidentally, perhaps, France had recently become a net contributor to the commission's budget, paying in more than its farmers got back in the form of agricultural subsidies.)

Though still strongly indebted to their rural constituencies, European politicians were beginning to worry as much about how to pay for growing problems like unemployment and urban blight as about how to prop up an archaic, even inefficient family-farm economy. "In the past five years, unemployed populations have become more important than agricultural populations," said Vonthron of the European Commission. "There's more demand to spend money on the future than to give it to a sector that is modern in some parts, not so modern in others."

The United States had mainly the European Community in mind when it submitted its sweeping plan to rid the world of agricultural subsidies. The Common Market countries are the principal importers of many U.S. farm goods; they are also the United States' main competitors in other markets. And along with the United States, they use an array of clearly predatory policies to protect their own farmers and get rid of their surpluses. "We hit them one. They hit us one. We're just slugging it out," said de la Garza. "It's not worth the effort of fighting all the time. Neither they nor we can keep on spending the levels of money that we've been spending."

The United States and Europe are not the only ones subsidizing their farmers. Japan would spend $10.5 billion on agriculture in 1988. Canada's farm-program costs would reach $1.5 billion. Canada and Australia, in particular, feared that their

E. "Kiki" de la Garza, D-Texas, served as chairman of the House Agriculture Committee.

treasuries could be bankrupted if a full-scale subsidy war broke out between the United States and the Europeans.

Stagnant Markets

Another reason the United States and other exporting nations are ready to negotiate a truce in farm subsidies is the shrinking market for their products. Commercial demand for food and fiber is nowhere near as large as the world's abundant supply, and many governments are looking for ways to protect their market shares.

World agricultural production expanded sharply in the 1950s and 1960s as industrial countries rebounded from World War II. The massive disruption of shipping during the war put added emphasis on self-sufficiency in agriculture and on expanding domestic production, especially in Britain, Western Europe, and Japan. Then during the 1970s, world consumption of farm products shot up. Rising incomes led to improved diets and higher consumption of meat, poultry, and dairy products. Demand outran supply in the early 1970s, particularly when the Soviet Union jumped into the world grain market with mammoth purchases. Total imports around the world grew from 285 million metric tons in 1970 to nearly 500 million metric tons by 1980. In a rather short period, the Soviet Union, Japan, and a host of developing countries became the major importers of food. It was supplied mainly by the United States and Europe. (See Figure 8-1.)

But in 1982, a worldwide recession tipped world trade in most agricultural products to a sudden crash. Economic and trade growth slowed, but world agricultural production continued to climb. Several countries had by this time enacted policies designed to encourage agricultural production, much of it intended to meet a rising export demand that no longer existed. According to some estimates, world farm productivity in the mid-1980s was increasing by 2.4 percent a year, double the rate of population and income growth. Without substantial acreage cutbacks or a big increase in food demand, experts said, agricultural production would soon overwhelm the world's storehouses.

Global food production exceeded annual demand by a fourth. The surplus grain stocks in the United States would feed the country for nearly a year. Europe has built a "butter mountain" with its dairy surpluses, which total 1.68 million metric

Figure 8-1   World Crop Trade

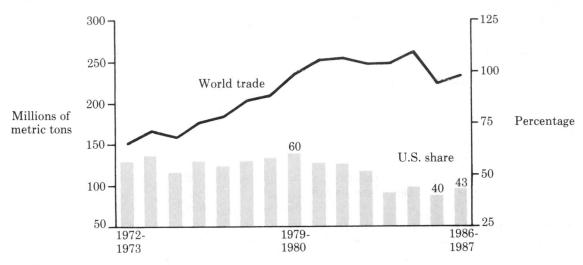

Source: U.S. Department of Agriculture, Economic Research Service.
Note: World crop trade of wheat, coarse grains, and soybeans.

tons—more weight, noted U.S. Under Secretary of State Allen Wallis, "than the entire population of Belgium, the Netherlands and Luxembourg combined."

European exports have continued to expand, but only with the help of direct export subsidies. Canada, Australia, and Argentina encouraged and expanded their grain exports. India, Pakistan, Saudi Arabia, and Great Britain, which had been major importers in the 1970s, all became wheat exporters by the 1980s. China became a corn exporter. Pakistan, Taiwan, China, and Indonesia became rice exporters, nearly all while facing large internal malnutrition problems.

The U.S. share of grain export markets fell precipitously, from a high of nearly 52 percent of the world market in 1981 to 32 percent in 1986. The European Community's share, on the other hand, rose from 17 percent to 25 percent during the same period. The Common Agricultural Policy, designed in the 1950s to shore up domestic prices at a time when the European Community was a net importer of agricultural products, had quickly taken on the primary function of encouraging European farmers to grow for export, at highly subsidized prices.

As a result, the United States stepped up its own export promotions in 1985, putting even more downward pressure on prices as U.S. exporters tried to regain their old market shares. The 1985 farm bill allowed prices of major commodities to fall by 25 percent to 50 percent, though it protected farmers with a cushion of income subsidies. Congress also ordered the administration to push U.S. exports with aggressive credit and direct-subsidy programs, and, after some early White House protests about subsidizing the Communist government of the Soviet Union and otherwise engaging in unfair trading practices, the administration willingly complied.

In 1988, for the first time in three years, the Soviet Union was expected to jump back into the grain market in a big way, buying up as much as $1.9 billion in U.S. wheat, corn, soybeans, and other commodities, nearly three times more than in 1987. Sales of almost four million metric tons of wheat were covered by subsidies under the United States' Export Enhancement Program (EEP), which pays generic PIK certificates to U.S. exporters who agree to lower their prices enough to match or better other export subsidizing nations. Between May 1985 and September 1987, EEP sales to all countries totaled close to eighteen million metric tons of wheat and wheat products, more than three million tons of barley, and smaller quantities of other commodities. The 1986 PIK payments averaged about $25 a ton for wheat and just under $80 a ton for wheat flour. Through 1988, the program as a whole was expected to provide at least $1 billion in PIK certificates to U.S. exporters.

European Community officials complained that EEP was an illegal subsidy program because it targeted and, in their opinion, undercut world prices. The community made a determined effort to protect what it considered its markets by providing increased subsidies to countries that had been targeted by the United States under the EEP. Argentina, Australia, and Canada also were adversely affected by the U.S. subsidy program. Despite assurances from the Reagan administration that the program would be used in a way that would avoid hurting these nonsubsidizing countries, the decision to make EEP available to the Soviet Union put the United States in direct competition with these trading allies.

"Other countries are often perceived in Congress as the unmitigated villains, and the United States as the only one willing to do something [about cutting farm subsidies]," said Timothy Mackey, agriculture counselor at the Australian embassy in Washington. "But in the United States, there haven't been any steps taken to reduce agriculture subsidies. If anything, U.S. export subsidies have increased."

Farm Subsidies

Governments employ a wide range of devices to protect farmers from the vagaries of the marketplace. Some, like tariffs and export subsidies, are direct, clearly protectionist efforts to control imports and exports. Others, such as price supports, are indirect and less obvious in the way they affect production, consumption, and trade in agriculture. Most countries say it is their sovereign right to have whatever kind of domestic policies they want. Nevertheless, nearly all of the agricultural policies would be under discussion at the new GATT round.

Some of the most common agricultural supports are:

Variable Levies. The cornerstone of the European Economic Community's Common Agricultural Policy, a variable levy makes up the difference between the price of an imported farm product delivered at the port and an official price at which foreign goods can be sold. It is effectively a tax on imports, constantly adjusted to make the imported product noncompetitive with the corresponding domestic product. Variable levies are also used by non-Common Market countries in Europe, such as Austria, Sweden, and Switzerland.

Export Restitutions. Many governments resort to export subsidies to dispose of surpluses. The European Community provides export restitutions almost automatically if world prices fall below domestic prices. The United States also uses export subsidies through the EEP as well as by offering credit guarantees on certain exports.

Tariffs. Less common in agricultural trade than variable levies, fixed tariffs or taxes on imports are used most often for protecting processed food. One of the tenets of GATT is that protection of domestic industries should come only through customs tariffs, not through nontariff measures such as quotas. That is designed to make protective policies "transparent," or obvious, to all trading partners, and thus easier to curb through negotiations.

Import Quotas. Used by most countries, these are most commonly imposed on dairy, sugar, beef, vegetables, and fruits to restrict imports at a specified quantity or value. Japan's agriculture policy limits access on twenty-two agricultural items, including rice, wheat, and beef. A government agency in Japan has exclusive authority to buy all internal production from farmers, and also all imports. The agency sets the price it will pay for each commodity, making the local price for rice, for instance, as much as eight times the world price.

The United States obtained a special waiver during previous GATT rounds to apply import barriers on a wide range of agricultural products. The president imposes these fees and quotas under the so-called Section 22 provision of U.S. farm law.

Production Quotas. Used in the United States mainly for milk, peanuts, and tobacco, and in Europe for dairy products, production quotas are government-organized franchises granting a farmer the right to sell a specified quantity of a crop at a guaranteed price. They guarantee a high price for domestic production but often require the use of import barriers to keep out cheaper foreign goods.

Price Supports, Target Prices. In nearly every industrial country, the government offers to buy certain domestically produced farm commodities at a fixed price. The United States buys dairy products directly, but for grain farmers it offers price-support "loans" at harvest, at predetermined per-bushel prices. Farmers use their crops as collateral for the loans, and if they cannot get a better price at the market than the loan rate, they can forfeit their crops and keep the principal. Cotton and rice farmers can get a "marketing loan" that allows them to repay their loans at whatever price their crops bring at the market and pocket the difference. In addition to price-support loans, Congress sets a higher "target" price for major crops, paying farmers a "deficiency payment" to cover the difference between the target price and the loan rate.

State Marketing Boards. Government-controlled trading agencies control 90 percent of world wheat trade and 70 percent of feed-grain trade. Canada, Australia, and New Zealand use marketing boards to sell domestic products at competitive prices in world markets. As world prices have fallen, however, some have had to make up the losses with direct government payments.

Transport. Canada has a unique policy dating from 1897, when the government subsidized a railroad through Crow's Nest Pass in the Rocky Mountains. The railroads agreed to freeze their freight rates for transporting wheat and feed grains to the ports for export. By 1981-1982, farmers were paying only one-sixth the cost of freight. The government has begun to revise the Crow's Nest system so that by 1990 farmers will be paying half the cost themselves.

Consumer Subsidies. Some Eastern-bloc countries that allow farm prices to remain high subsidize the price at the grocery store.

Health and Safety. Regulations propagated in the name of consumer health and safety also may affect what can be traded. A World Bank study in four countries found that health standards affected 95 percent of food imports into Japan, 94 percent in Norway, 60 percent in Australia, and 55 percent in Switzerland.

International Tensions

The increasing reliance on predatory export policies and other farm subsidies has only increased political tensions among the world's major trading nations. The hardest hit were countries that depended heavily on agricultural exports to bring positive returns in their national trade balances but were not in the habit of spending a lot of money to subsidize farmers. U.S. grain subsidies prompted Australian leaders to question their continued commitment to U.S. defense installations in their country. U.S. sugar policy has slowed imports from debt-ridden Latin American countries, shutting off their main source of cash and threatening the continued success of the multinational Caribbean Basin Initiative. Argentina, Canada, and Thailand have been among those protesting the loudest to U.S. policy makers about the loss of their export markets. Many officials in the United States and abroad fear the growing unease could spread to other industries and lead to a major trade war.

Since 1986, leaders around the world began to join the United States in calls to bring agriculture under some form of trade order. Trade ministers from seventy-four countries met in Punta del Este, Uruguay, in September 1986 and agreed to launch a new round of GATT negotiations. Agriculture was made a major agenda item, along with intellectual property rights, services, and investment. In May 1987, a group of twenty-five, mostly Western industrial countries, the Organization for Economic Cooperation and Development (OECD), agreed at a ministerial meeting in Paris to negotiate a reduction

in agricultural subsidies. At the Venice economic summit in June 1987, Reagan made agriculture a primary agenda item. The reception was cooler than desired, but the leaders of the seven largest Western industrial countries issued a communiqué on agriculture that, while setting no firm dates, at least promised to negotiate reforms.

U.S. farmers have come to rely on foreign sales for much of their income. Here wheat is loaded on barges in Pendleton, Ore., for shipment overseas.

GATT Background

For the time being, at least, talks on agriculture would take place under the auspices of the GATT. Formal negotiations in Geneva, at the so-called Uruguay Round (named after the Punta del Este meeting at which trade ministers agreed to meet), began in January 1988. Other trade-related items on the Uruguay Round agenda included intellectual property rights, services, and investments—controversial issues that could take years to work out. But the administration pushed for what it called an "early harvest" on agriculture, in the hope of bringing home an agreement before Reagan left office.

Established in 1947, the General Agreement on Tariffs and Trade was designed to prevent a recurrence of the trade conflicts of 1930s, which contributed to the outbreak of World War II. There have been seven previous negotiating rounds; the most recent was the lengthy Tokyo Round of 1973 to 1979, when agriculture for the first time became a separate item on the agenda. Most GATT rounds were more successful in liberalizing industrial trade than agricultural trade. The member countries, or contracting parties, of the GATT agree to its code of principles and rules for trade. The GATT also provides a framework for settling disputes.

One of the basic tenets of the GATT is nondiscrimination and reciprocity in trade, which means member countries must grant each other such favorable treatment as they give to any single country. The main tool for enforcing that tenet is a "bound duty." Negotiated tariff levels are "bound" in GATT; that is, one country guarantees it will not raise a tariff without renegotiation, consultation, and usually compensation, which can only happen every three years.

But GATT restrictions are only loosely applied to agriculture, especially when it involves the other important tenet that protection of domestic industries should avoid the use of quotas and be limited to transparent duties, such as customs tariffs. Special exceptions to the nontariff protection ban have effectively negated its application to agriculture. The GATT also prohibits export subsidies—but here, too, it has made an exception for agriculture so that member countries must simply "seek to avoid" using them.

In 1955, GATT granted the United States a special waiver to apply import barriers on a wide range of agricultural products. The waiver permits fees or quotas on imported farm products if they would undermine domestic farm programs. The president may impose fees and quotas under Section 22 of permanent farm law, established in 1933.

This GATT waiver for the United States established a precedent for other members to use similar techniques to protect their own farm sectors. "Instead of developing domestic agricultural policies to fit the rules of GATT, we have tried to develop rules to fit the policies," noted Dale Hathaway, a former under secretary of agriculture and author of a study on

160

agriculture and the GATT. "Not only did agriculture receive special treatment in GATT, but special treatment appears to be tailored to U.S. farm programs."

The United States also won an important concession in previous GATT negotiations that may play a role in the current round. In the Dillon Round of 1960-1961, the United States wanted guaranteed access to Europe for grains, a concession the community refused to grant. However, the community did grant a duty-free binding for soybean oil products and other nongrain feed exports (soybean meal, tapioca, corn gluten, and citrus pulp) into Europe. The effect of no duties or levies on soybean imports represented a value of only $700 million at the time. But soybean imports eventually grew to a peak of $2.5 billion in 1980, mostly from the United States. The EC now wants to renegotiate the soybean agreement to limit imports from the United States.

There are a number of structural limitations to the GATT that many observers believe would make it difficult to reach an agreement, particularly a quick agreement sought by the Reagan administration. Not least is the decline of the multilateral principal since the GATT was formed. Governments frustrated with agricultural trade distortions have begun in recent years to seek out limited, bilateral deals. This trend to bilateralism has entailed a greater use of import barriers and export subsidies, the very techniques GATT generally prohibits.

In addition, most GATT members do not want to negotiate on import barriers, such as quotas, variable levies, and voluntary export restraints, because they touch on domestic programs. It would require the United States, for instance, to put its special Section 22 waiver on the bargaining table. U.S. commodities protected under Section 22 import quotas are peanuts, cotton, and dairy products—commodities that are represented by some of the strongest regional factions in Congress, and which together account for 7 percent of world trade. Other commodity interests not now protected by Section 22's duties or quotas do not want its provisions weakened for fear that their day to seek protection could come.

Major Players

By virtue of their agriculture export and import volumes, the United States and the European Economic Community are the principal antagonists at the new GATT talks in Geneva. Together they control most of the world's trade in agricultural products, and they spend the most money to support their farmers. "They are the elephants," said George Rossmiller, director of the National Center for Food and Agricultural Policy, Resources for the Future.

The European Community has come a long way from the old agreement among the original six members, who formed in 1957 and basically traded industrial protections in West Germany for agricultural protections in France. The Common Agricultural Policy essentially adopted and institutionalized the market-intervention policies long in place in both those countries. Conceived as a way to stabilize internal prices, the CAP provides for absolute preference for member producers and common funding for farm programs through the European Commission in Brussels, Belgium. The CAP also provides common prices for agricultural products in all member countries, and given the wide disparities in farm size, land structure, and rural populations of the members, the common prices remain high enough to satisfy the highest-cost, or least efficient, producers. The EC budget is paid for from the variable import levy, plus a value-added tax collected by member governments.

The European Community has undergone a large shift in agricultural production since 1980, bringing the CAP under new criticism. For twenty years, between 1960 and 1980, the community was a net importer of wheat and course grains, but it has since become a net exporter. In 1976, the expanded ten-member community had net imports of twenty-five million metric tons of grain. By 1984, it had net exports of nineteen million tons, a total turnaround of forty-four million tons in nine years.

Export subsidies are the most sensitive issue for the European Community. When the Europeans joined the talks, they would not agree to a statement that singled out the central elements of their Common Agricultural Policy. Instead, the declaration talked broadly about phasing out the "negative effects" of direct and indirect subsidies. This allows the United States to talk about the CAP in Geneva, but it also lets the Europeans focus on certain U.S. programs—Food for Peace (PL 480), export "enhancement," and export credit guarantees—that effectively subsidize U.S. farm shipments overseas.

Japan, the other significant force in agricultural trade talks, is the largest importer of agricultural products, accounting for 9 percent of world trade. But as a net importer, Japan says its policies do not inhibit export competition. World War II left Japan with two abiding concerns in agriculture: a lasting desire for self-sufficiency (particularly in rice), created by a wartime food shortage; and a political system that gives disproportionate weight in the Japanese Diet, or parliament, to rural voters, who are the main constituency of the ruling Liberal Democratic party.

Rice is the only crop on half of Japanese farms and accounts for one-third of farm income. Nominal prices in 1986 declined for the first time since the 1950s, and Japanese rice farmers are now producing more than their consumers can eat. While the Japanese have shown restraint in the use of export subsidies (under pressure from the United States), the last thing the government wants to do is import rice. "Deep down, the Japanese wish they'd be left alone, and that these negotiations would go away," said Michael Lopez of the Agriculture Department's Economic Research Service.

For that and other reasons, Japan is not expected to be an active participant in early GATT negotiations. U.S. trade officials expect the Japanese will let the United States and the European Community haggle over agriculture issues, then decide whether to sign any agreement reached. Japan may even prefer to seek separate bilateral deals with individual countries instead of taking part in a multilateral GATT agreement. What may in the end bring the Japanese into the negotiations is if agriculture falls apart and, as a result, the whole GATT round falls apart. "That will bother them," said Lynn Condon of the U.S. trade representative's office. "If everybody starts doing their own thing, the target for 90 percent of the retaliatory trade policies will be Japan. They know that."

Another important faction in the negotiations is a group of thirteen agricultural exporting countries, led by Australia, that has submitted its own proposal for reducing agricultural subsidies. The others in this so-called Cairnes Group are Argentina, Brazil, Canada, Chile, Colombia, Hungary, Indonesia, Malaysia, New Zealand, the Philippines, Thailand, and Uruguay. While they represent a mix of big and small nations, developed and developing economies, most are agricultural exporters concerned about the rising use of subsidies. "We see ourselves as the most significant third force in the negotiations," said Timothy Mackey of the Australian embassy. "We're too big to be ignored by the EC and the United States, even if we're too small to bash them into submission."

A Single Yardstick

To bring the various agricultural interests and policies under a single rubric, the United States has proposed that GATT negotiators use a new gauge of agricultural subsidies—a producer subsidy equivalent, or PSE. Put simply, a PSE is what a country would have to pay a farmer to give up a subsidy. If a country's PSE is 10 percent, for instance, it means that government subsidies are equal to 10 percent of a farmer's income. (See Figure 8-2.)

A U.S. Department of Agriculture study showed that Japan had the highest overall PSE; its agricultural policies accounted for 70 percent of farmers' incomes. The European Community's PSE was 33 percent, followed by the United States at 22 percent, and Australia at 9 percent.

The advantage of PSEs is their comparability across nations and commodities. They can measure both direct subsidies, such as U.S. income supports, and indirect ones, such as Japanese import barriers. A big drawback is their reliance on incomplete data and different collection methods.

Studies by the World Bank, the OECD, and the Agriculture Department show that in general, liberalized trading conditions would help boost prices of farm goods, presumably because farmers would begin to produce for actual market conditions and reduce production in commodities with low demand. That means the winners and losers of trade liberalization, as measured by PSEs, would vary from country to country and commodity to commodity.

In the United States, income gains could be made in feed grains and oilseeds, but not so much in livestock, dairy, and wheat. In general, the biggest gains would go to the low-cost producers who could still make a profit without government subsidies or import protections. Income losses would be large in Europe and Japan, where small, inefficient farms are being propped up by the governments. And since the Cairnes Group countries do not spend much money for agriculture subsidies, their farmers would be big gainers under an agreement that liberalized trade and boosted prices for farm products.

In general, overall producer welfare in industrialized coun-

Figure 8-2 Producer Subsidy Equivalents

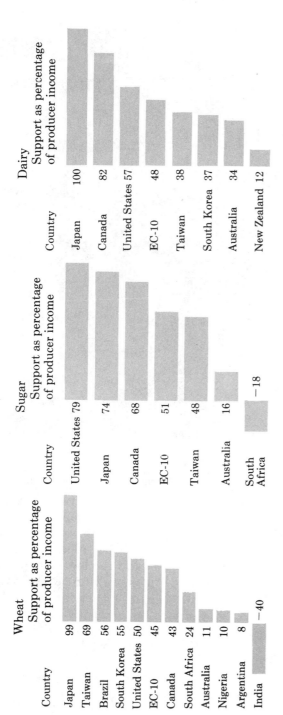

Wheat

Country	Support as percentage of producer income
Japan	99
Taiwan	69
Brazil	56
South Korea	55
United States	50
EC-10	45
Canada	43
South Africa	24
Australia	11
Nigeria	10
Argentina	8
India	−40

Sugar

Country	Support as percentage of producer income
United States	79
Japan	74
Canada	68
EC-10	51
Taiwan	48
Australia	16
South Africa	−18

Dairy

Country	Support as percentage of producer income
Japan	100
Canada	82
United States	57
EC-10	48
Taiwan	38
South Korea	37
Australia	34
New Zealand	12

Source: U.S. Department of Agriculture, Economic Research Service.

Note: Data are 1985-1986 average. EC-10= Membership of the European Economic Community (Common Market) before the entrance of Spain and Portugal.

The elimination of farm subsidies would mean lower prices for Japanese shoppers.

tries would be reduced by $55.6 billion. Producers in developing countries, on the other hand, would gain $27.8 billion. Consumers in industrial countries would be the biggest gainers, saving about $101.1 billion, with most of the gains coming in Europe and Japan, where farm policies keep food prices artificially high. (U.S. farm policy, on the other hand, relies mainly on budget expenditures; consumers already get low food prices.) Consumer losers would be those in Eastern Europe, the Soviet Union, and practically all developing countries, where government policies serve to keep grocery prices artificially low.

New Markets

Budget pressures may have pushed many of the agricultural producing nations to the bargaining table, but they also invite quick-fix remedies. What may keep the United States, the European Community, and the Cairnes Group countries bargaining for more than just short-term solutions is another mutual, long-term interest they have in agriculture.

Agricultural trade experts generally believe that the future of agriculture for industrial exporting nations lies not in their own trading relationships, but in potential new markets of the Third World. The European Community and Canada now purchase about 25 percent of all U.S. farm exports. But in the recent past, developing countries actually represented a faster-growing market for the United States. During the boom years between 1975 and 1980, the share of U.S. agricultural exports that went to developing countries grew from 30 percent to 35 percent. The recession and concurrent Third World debt problems since 1981 halted that expansion; according to the Agriculture Department, eighteen countries that are major markets for the United States hold more than 60 percent of the problem debt. "That's what keeps us negotiating," said Daniel Amstutz, a former under secretary of agriculture under Reagan and the administration's chief negotiator on agriculture in the Uruguay Round of GATT.

Yet Third World imports grow only if those nations experience significant economic development. In the 1970s, imports of wheat and coarse grains by developing countries increased from 20.4 million tons to 58.6 million tons. More than 70 percent of the imports were by upper-middle-income countries, where rapid increases in per capita incomes were occurring. Many agricultural economists believe the development of an agricultural industry is the key to economic growth in developing countries. The main natural resources of these countries are agricultural, and increasing productivity in agriculture would be the key to raising overall incomes. "There's damn little to negotiate between us and the EC until we start to expand the agenda," said G. Edward Schuh, former director of agriculture and rural development at the World Bank in Washington. "That's why it's important to get the developing countries engaged."

Promoting agricultural development is a controversial issue among U.S. farmers, who generally believe that helping developing countries expand their agricultural output will only result in more competition for the United States. But case studies in a few developing countries suggest that once poor populations begin to experience economic gains from local agricultural production, demand for other types of food—especially meat and fine grain products—goes up.

Brazilian agriculture, for example, doubled in value between 1970 and 1985, increasing nearly 7 percent a year, one of the highest growth rates in the world, said the World Bank's Schuh. Although Brazil competes with the United States in soybean meal and oil, its overall imports of U.S. farm products increased by 15 percent a year in quantity and 25 percent in value.

India was often mentioned as a "lost market" for agriculture as result of international assistance and the "Green Revolution," which brought the country to self-sufficiency in wheat and even enabled it to become a small net exporter of wheat. But most of the displaced imports were food aid shipments under the U.S. Food for Peace program. India still has millions of poor and undernourished, which means the country's self-sufficiency may stem from the population's inability to buy. The U.S. Agriculture Department estimates that 50 percent of the population of India cannot afford a nutritional diet.

At the GATT, the interests of developing countries are taken seriously by the European Community. The so-called ACP countries—African, Caribbean, and Pacific—are former colonies of France and Britain. These countries already benefit from some preferential trade treatment, but their agricultural exports might be greater if the major industrial countries cut back on their protectionist policies. "Each country wants to gain in these developing markets, but they're not sure if they really exist," said the European Commission's Vonthron.

The United States also is paying close attention to developing countries in the new GATT round. Many are skeptical of U.S. intentions. "India and Brazil are suspicious," said Amstutz, who is heading the U.S. negotiating team on agriculture in Geneva. "They've been burned by our domestic programs, and not just in agriculture; the Indians think we want to take over their banking system.

"But Third World countries are our natural allies in this process," Amstutz added. "It's up to us to convince them that eliminating farm subsidies means their agriculture can expand, that it can generate foreign exchange and that they can get rid of their debt. Then they can make better customers for the United States."

Possible Outcomes

The political and structural problems with the GATT suggest that much less ambitious results than the complete elimination of subsidies proposed by the Reagan administration will come out of the negotiating process. Because domestic policies produce surpluses and trade distortions, any agreement to reduce subsidies would require a reduction in local price and income supports, an unlikely prospect in either the United States, Europe, or Japan. However, there is a move in the current GATT round to discuss the "effects" of domestic policies, not the policies themselves. That might allow some of the most protective governments to join a deal that puts limits on agricultural subsidies without saying exactly how.

But since the GATT members are negotiating agriculture, manufacturing, and services on separate tracks, it will be difficult to exchange concessions from one track to another and thus allow a loser in agriculture to come out a winner in manufacturing or services. "That probably preordains a fairly limited amount of trade liberalization," said Schuh.

A more likely outcome, then, would involve less ambitious ways to control agricultural trade subsidies than the Draconian method suggested by the Reagan administration. Some possible outcomes could include a variation on one or more of the following:

Market-Sharing Agreements. GATT might produce a "wheat cartel," or other commodity-by-commodity bargain. Such an accord is an important goal of developing countries, and many analysts believe the Europeans also have a predilection for the "management" of markets rather than letting them operate by supply and demand.

But market-sharing could be unworkable, many trade experts said. Major trading nations, mainly the United States, Australia, Canada, and Argentina, would find it unacceptable in principle and could refuse to participate. In past GATT rounds, negotiators came up with a wheat agreement that attempted to manage both price and quantity, but it soon broke down under market pressures. Other market-sharing attempts were made for meats and dairy, and they also failed. "The world is littered with the remains of international commodity agreements that have not worked," said Hathaway, author of a study on agriculture and the GATT talks for the Institute for International

Economics.

Cartels are also hard to negotiate. An important question would be whether the negotiated market shares for the United States and the European Community would be at their 1980 levels, when the United States had the advantage, or at the figures recorded in 1985, which would give an edge to the Europeans.

World Set-Asides. One way to achieve the effect of market-sharing is with a global acreage-reduction scheme, much like the United States uses to encourage farmers to limit output. This could find some favor in Congress. Dan Glickman, D-Kan., chairman of the House Agriculture Subcommittee on Wheat, Soybeans and Feed Grains, said world set-asides would be one way to get an "informal" market-sharing agreement without resorting to an outright cartel. "I think we're after an agreement to reduce subsidies," Glickman said. "I don't think we can do that without having some implicit agreement to share markets. I'm not talking about a cartel. But we have to have cooperation, an implicit understanding of markets and historical relationships."

Subsidy Freeze. The Cairnes Group called for an immediate freeze on new agricultural subsidies as a way to set the stage for more permanent reductions. But even after promising to negotiate for reductions, the United States and other countries pushed to expand export subsidies. The House and Senate Agriculture committees each voted to increase export subsidies in their sections of a comprehensive trade bill (HR 3), which was adopted by Congress in April 1988 but vetoed by President Reagan for reasons unrelated to its agriculture provisions. The European Community proposed a new tax on fats and oils. And Canadians increased certain subsidies to their producers.

Bilateral Agreements. Many experts see a potential in GATT for two or three of the dominant traders to strike deals that would serve their interests in given commodities. The United States and Japan cut just such a deal on the eve of the June 1988 Toronto economic summit. Japan promised easier access for U.S. citrus and beef but also neutralized Reagan's broader agriculture agenda at Toronto. "The greatest danger in these negotiations is that the two most powerful participants, the EC and the United States, will reach accommodations that meet their most pressing political needs without dealing with the basic issues," Hathaway said.

Dan Glickman, D-Kan., chairman of the Agriculture Subcommittee on Wheat, Soybeans and Feed Grains, was an advocate of world set-asides.

"Historians would call it a return to mercantilism," Amstutz added.

Back to Congress

Even if U.S. trade negotiators can strike a deal overseas, no one, least of all the Reagan administration, could be sure that Congress would suddenly find the political will to enact the necessary legislation to cut federal farm subsidies. "The concerns on the part of foreigners are whether we can sell it to Congress," acknowledged Assistant U.S. Trade Representative Condon. "But the real problem is whether we can sell it to our farm groups. I don't see any distinction between farm groups and Congress."

Amstutz said farm groups and farm-state lawmakers would respond positively to a negotiated cut in subsidies, so long as they were made to feel informed and part of the process. And Democratic leaders on the House and Senate Agriculture committees have given the administration high marks for keeping the communication lines open. In any case, the administration's emphasis on agriculture in the GATT virtually assured that Congress would have little to do on farm legislation until the current five-year farm bill expires in 1990. Even then, farm-state members might not want to tinker with farm law if GATT negotiations were showing any signs of progress.

Meanwhile, farm-state members of Congress were basking in a new political climate in Washington. The free-market Reagan administration finally adopted their view that the United States cannot afford to change its farm policy unless foreign competitors play along. "We are clearly not going to reduce our level of government involvement [in agriculture] unless other people move with us," said U.S. Trade Representative Yeutter in July 1987. "We are going to go down this road together, and we are going to go down it arm in arm, and we are not going to walk ten steps ahead of the Europeans or the Japanese or anybody else."

Until that international convergence occurs, the arena for making big changes in governmental farm programs will remain in Geneva—far from the U.S. Congress and farther still from the American farmer.

Appendix A

Commodity Programs

United States farm law is a grab bag of policies designed to bolster the prices of various commodities and support the incomes of their producers. Most price-support programs for major commodities were last reauthorized by Congress in 1985 as part of omnibus legislation (PL 99-198) to revise and extend agriculture and nutrition programs. The bill reauthorized programs for five years, so current programs will be expiring at the end of 1990.

As in the past, the bill amended and added to—but did not repeal—permanent farm policy legislation of 1938 and 1949.

Here is a summary of the major sections of the bill and the various policies the government uses to support the prices of U.S. commodities and the incomes of American farmers.

Wheat and Feed Grains

The core of U.S. farm policy deals with price and income-supports for wheat, corn, and other feed grains, mainly because those commodities consume most of the federal outlays for farm programs. They also took the brunt of depressed economic conditions in agriculture in the mid-1980s.

The wheat and feed grains programs enacted in 1985 (and modified only slightly since then) were a carefully crafted compromise between the Reagan administration's goal of reducing the artificial floor the government puts on wheat and corn prices, and giving struggling farmers some cash security if prices continued to stay below the cost of production.

The most dramatic departure from previous farm law was a

provision in the bill to peg price-support "loan rates" to actual market fluctuations. In past years, Congress arbitrarily set loan rates on a rising scale, keeping an eye on inflation, with the result that those rates were generally higher than prices on most world markets. That led farmers to forfeit much of their crops to the government.

Under the 1985 bill, the basic wheat loan rate was dropped from $3.30 a bushel to $3.00 in 1986 and would be allowed to fall another 5 percent a year through 1990 depending on market conditions. Corn rates were dropped in similar fashion, from $2.55 a bushel to $2.40 in 1986.

Furthermore, the agriculture secretary was empowered—in some years, required—to reduce the rate another 20 percent a year. That took the loan rates to $2.21 for wheat and $1.77 for corn by 1988, much closer to the prevailing world prices and making it more more difficult for foreign nations to undersell U.S. grain on overseas markets.

Cutting the loan rates, however, only served to widen the gap between market prices and "target prices," the mechanism used to determine how much the government would pay to farmers in the form of direct income subsidies. The 1985 farm bill resulted in a compromise that froze target prices for wheat and corn at their 1985 levels for two years, then allowed rates to drop a total of 10 percent over the remaining three years of the bill, in annual increments of 2 percent in 1988, 3 percent in 1989, and 5 percent in 1990. A 1987 amendment further reduced the 1988 and 1989 rates by another 1.4 percent, bringing target prices to $4.23 for wheat and $2.93 for corn in 1988.

As a condition of receiving government price- and income-supports, wheat and feed grain farmers had to comply with certain acreage reduction requirements as determined annually by the agriculture secretary. For wheat, the acreage reduced ranged from a minimum of 20 percent of a farmer's established wheat acreage base to a maximum of 30 percent. For feed grains, the minimum acreage reduction was 12.5 percent and the maximum 20 percent.

To further encourage production cutbacks, wheat and feed grains farmers were given an option to plant only 50 percent of their base acreage and still get 92 percent of the expected income-support benefits. That "50-92" scheme was expanded to a "0-92" option in the 1987 legislation, allowing farmers to plant nothing and still get 92 percent of their benefits.

Cotton and Rice

Although cotton and rice farmers are a smaller group than other commodity interests, legislators representing Southern states where cotton and rice are grown played a proportionately larger role in the 1985 farm bill debate than any other special interest. As a result, the cotton and rice programs contained some of the most charitable price-support provisions in the entire package.

Southern lawmakers used their senior positions on the Agriculture committees to win passage for a radical new kind of price-support mechanism for cotton and rice farmers, called a "marketing loan." The plan called for the government to issue crop loans to farmers at low interest rates, much like wheat and feed grain programs, but with a key difference: Instead of allowing farmers to default on their loans and turn over their crops to the government if prices fall below the loan rate, the agriculture secretary had to allow rice and cotton farmers to pay back only as much as they could get on the open market. The farmer-borrowers who sold their crops at a lower rate could keep the remaining principal from the loan.

A big advantage of marketing loans was a congressionally mandated exemption from payment limitations that applied to recipients of deficiency payments under the wheat and feed grain programs.

The farm bill maintained the existing loan-rate formula for cotton at 85 percent of average market prices, limiting reduction to a maximum of 5 percent a year. It placed a floor of fifty cents per pound on loans rates from 1987 through 1990. The cotton loan rate was about fifty-two cents a pound in 1988.

As with wheat and feed grains, target prices for cotton were frozen—at eighty-one cents a pound in 1986 and reduced a total of 10 percent over the life of the bill (with further reductions enacted in 1988). The target price for cotton was about seventy-six cents in 1988. Acreage reduction requirements were capped at 25 percent of a farmer's established cotton base.

Loan rates for rice were allowed to fall gradually from $8.00 a hundredweight (one-hundred pounds) in 1985, but to no less than $6.50. Target prices went from $11.90 per hundredweight to as low as $10.71 in 1990. Acreage reduction requirements could reach as high as 35 percent of a rice farmer's established base.

Soybeans

Technically, this is a "non-program" crop, since the government requires no acreage-reduction conditions and offers no income supports for soybean farmers. But the Agriculture Department does offer nonrecourse crop loans, which work the same way as wheat and feed grains. The loan rate was set at $5.02 a bushel in 1986 and 1987 and allowed to fall as much as 5 percent a year afterwards, though to no lower than $4.50. The 1988 soybean loan rate was $4.77.

Dairy

Unlike the other commodity programs, the government makes direct purchases of dairy products to support the price and remove surpluses from the market. This is accomplished by buying milk equivalents (butter, cheese, dry milk) from dairy cooperative processors at prices established by Congress. The 1985 farm bill held the dairy support price at $11.60 per hundredweight through 1986, then to $11.35 in January 1987, and $11.10 in October 1987. Further cuts were pegged to the amount of surplus production—another fifty cents a year if government purchases were projected to exceed 5 billion pounds. In 1988 the dairy support price was $10.60 per hundredweight.

The dairy industry won its biggest victory over the Reagan administration in 1985 when Congress approved a new program to reduce milk surpluses by requiring the government to buy up entire herds of dairy cows. The farm bill required the agriculture secretary to accept bids from dairy producers to send to slaughter or sell for export their entire dairy herds, calves and bulls included. The farmers had to agree to stay out of the diary business for five years.

The buyout experiment was paid for in part by assessments on all dairy producers, to be subtracted from their price-support checks. But Congress limited the assessments to forty cents per hundredweight in 1986 and twenty-five cents per hundredweight in 1987, forcing the government to make up the difference. The whole-herd buyout program, in effect for eighteen months beginning in April 1986, ultimately removed 1.3 million of the nation's 11 million dairy cows from milk production, reducing government purchases from 13.2 million pounds in 1985 to 6.7 million pounds in 1987. That was still not enough to avoid a fifty-cent cut in price-supports in 1988. Furthermore, milk production was expected to rebound to a record level in 1988, prompting critics to claim that the buyout effort was little more than a generous retirement bonus to older dairy farmers.

Sugar

Governmental intervention into sugar production and sugar trade is the oldest kind of farm policy in the United States. The first U.S. tariff on raw sugar was imposed in 1789, and the government has maintained import duties on sugar practically ever since.

From 1934 to 1974, U.S. sugar policy expanded to include production quotas, subjecting domestic producers to acreage restrictions, minimum wage, and child labor laws. These were combined with import quotas assigned to foreign countries, allowing the government to allocate virtually all domestic demand between domestic and foreign producers.

This system was not renewed in 1974, as sugar prices soared, but Congress again resorted to minimum support levels for sugar in the 1977 farm bill, and again in 1981 and 1985. The government now gives price-support loans to sugar processors, who agree to share the support price with sugar cane and beet producers. The loan rate is eighteen cents a pound for raw cane sugar, and a corresponding amount for beet sugar. As in grain programs, the processors use sugar as collateral for the loans and have the option of forfeiting the sugar to the government if domestic prices do not exceed the loan rate.

The 1985 farm bill added a new wrinkle to this system, much to the consternation of other sugar exporting nations (as well as the U.S. State and Treasury departments). That year Congress required the president to run the sugar program at no cost. The government had to assure that sugar supplies within the United States remained low enough to force domestic prices above the loan rate, and thus prevent the government from buying up the surplus. The only way to accomplish this was to impose stricter import quotas on countries that have traditionally supplied sugar to the United States.

One of the effects of this policy has been to keep domestic prices high enough for producers of sugar substitutes—particularly corn sweeteners—to expand their operations. Corn sweeteners would be less profitable for their manufacturers and less attractive to the soft drink industry if they were forced to compete with world sugar, which was priced in 1988 at about eight cents a pound.

Peanuts

There have been no basic changes in the peanut programs since 1948. The government maintains high domestic prices for peanuts through the use of increasingly tight production controls—including acreage allotments and marketing quotas—along with zero import quotas.

Prices are supported through loans to producer associations acting for farmers. In addition, the Agriculture Department purchases peanuts and diverts them from domestic food uses to alternative uses, such as oil and meal. The government also buys peanuts for export. The government absorbs the cost for selling these products at a lower price than the loan rate, which is based on the price of peanuts sold for the domestic food market. The 1985 farm bill set the loan rate at $559 a ton, allowing maximum increases of 6 percent a year. The 1988 peanut loan rate was $615.27 a ton.

Only those growers who hold marketing quotas for domestic sales are eligible for the support price, but then no peanuts are allowed to be sold for domestic consumption without a marketing quota and acreage allotment. As a result, a principal feature of the program is the increased value of land that comes to holders of these historical rights to plant and sell peanuts.

In 1985, Congress permitted farmers who did not hold a quota to sell peanuts for export or nonfood uses. It also gave the agriculture secretary discretion to provide price supports for these "additional" peanuts, at a rate of $149.75 a ton in 1988.

Honey

The marketing loan system used for cotton and rice producers is also available to honey producers, who may repay their price-support loans at less than the loan rate if market conditions are depressed. The loan rate for honey was fifty-nine cents a pound in 1988.

In 1986, Congress placed a $250,000 cap on federal loans to individual beekeepers. But it was quietly removed in late 1987, prompting urban critics to seek even tighter controls.

Wool and Mohair

Government programs protect domestic wool and mohair producers by giving them direct payments to supplement their incomes. Payments are based on the percentage needed to bring the average return (market price plus payment) up to an announced support level, based on average market prices. The support prices in 1988 were $1.78 a pound for shorn wool and $4.95 a pound for mohair.

Wool and mohair are deficit commodities in the United States, where much of the supply for apparel and carpet wool comes from imports. One of the main features of the program is to encourage the production and aggressive marketing of wool and mohair by aiming higher direct payments to producers to get higher market prices for their wool or mohair. There is also a duty on imported apparel wool, which helps give domestic wool a pricing advantage.

Tobacco

Congress in 1986 came up with a plan to salvage a controversial price-support program that tobacco-state legislators had believed was about to collapse. Tobacco has been supported by the government since 1933.

The tobacco program works much like the peanut program, offering nonrecourse price-support loans through producer associations, which handle payments from the government and also store surplus tobacco. The government uses a system of acreage allotments and marketing quotas in an effort to keep supplies in line with demand at market prices above the loan rate. Penalties for noncompliance are so severe that virtually all tobacco growers in the United States participate in the tobacco program. Holders of the historical acreage allotments also enjoy higher land values as a result.

Government surpluses mounted in the early 1980s as prices plunged on world markets. In 1982 Congress required growers to cover all loan program losses through assessments on tobacco sales. The assessments for the two main types of tobacco used in making cigarettes grew from three cents a pound in 1982 to twenty-five cents a pound for flue-cured tobacco and thirty cents a pound for burley tobacco in 1985. Many industry analysts were predicting that growers, who must hold a referendum on whether to continue the program, would choose to eliminate price supports altogether instead of continuing to pay for the program themselves.

Yearlong negotiations in 1985, organized by legislators in tobacco-growing states such as North Carolina and Kentucky, produced an agreement between growers and cigarette manufacturers. Enacted in 1986 as an amendment to another bill, the amended program lowered the federal price-support levels for various kinds of tobacco and provided for discounted sales of the huge surpluses the government had been forced to take over in recent years.

Cigarette companies agreed to share half the cost of the price-support program with growers and, in return, were allowed to buy up the existing surpluses for as little as 10 percent of their original value. The package also gave manufacturers a direct role in setting quotas on how much growers can grow and sell each year—and for how much foreign tobacco the cigarette companies could import.

In addition, tobacco-state legislators made the new program part of permanent farm law, thus ensuring they would not have to return to Congress for periodic reauthorizations.

Tobacco growers eventually voted to continue their price-support programs by overwhelming margins.

Appendix B

Glossary

The jargon used to discuss federal farm subsidies always has been rife with arcane terms describing rather Byzantine concepts. Farm-state lawmakers and "ag" experts freely throw these buzzwords around in the ongoing debate on federal agriculture policy. A few even admit that the code serves to shroud the inner workings of farm programs from confused urban critics.

As with any government program, however, the key to understanding esoteric concepts is to remember that most of them have to do with money. For example, one former Senate Agriculture Committee staffer, besieged with repeated requests for aid from various farm groups, offered this jaded reply one day when an inexperienced reporter asked him what was meant by the age-old agricultural term "parity."

"It's very simple," he said. "Parity means *more*."

Following is a guided tour through the peculiar lexicon of U.S. acriculture policy.

Acreage Reduction Program (ARP)—The main function of acreage reduction requirements is to control output. The ARP is a voluntary land retirement system in which farmers reduce their planted acreage from their base acreage. Under certain parameters set by Congress, the agriculture secretary each year proclaims acreage reduction targets for specified crops. The size of the reduction is determined by the amount that, combined with carryover from previous years and imports, will be needed to supply a normal year's domestic consumption, exports, and an allowance for reserves. Farmers are usually not paid for their ARP participation, although compliance with acreage reduction measures are usually made a condition for getting price- and income-supports and benefits of other farm programs.

Advance Crop Loans—Price-support loans made early in a crop year, as opposed to at harvestime. *See also* Nonrecourse Loans.

Base Acreage—For particular crops of wheat, feed grains, upland cotton, and rice, the average of the acreage planted and considered planted of the crop for harvest during the five preceding crop years. For particular farms, the total of the crop acreage bases for a particular year, plus the average acreage planted to soybeans, and the average acreage devoted to conserving uses (excluding ARPs).

Bilateral Agreement—A two-country agreement covering the general rules of trade or terms for the exchange of specified products. *See also* Multilateral Agreement.

Carryover—The supplies of a farm commodity not yet sold or otherwise disposed of at the end of a marketing year. Marketing years generally start at the beginning of the new harvest for a commodity.

Commodity Credit Corporation (CCC)—A wholly owned federal corporation within the U.S. Department of Agriculture. The CCC functions as the financial institution through which all money transactions are handled for farm price and income support.

Conservation Reserve Program (CRP)—A long-range program under which farmers voluntarily contract to take cropland out of production for ten to fifteen years and devote it to conserving uses, such as grasslands or trees. In return, farmers receive an annual rental payment for the contract period and assistance, either in cash or payment-in-kind (PIK), for carrying out approved conservation practices on the reserve acreage.

Cross-compliance—The restriction of benefits to those who complied with the acreage reduction and other requirements of all commodity programs applicable to a given farm, even if a farmer is actually participating in only one of those programs.

Decoupling—A proposal to remove the link between government farm payments and crop production. A farmer could choose to take income-support payments based on previous production of a particular crop, no matter what crop is planted in the future, or whether a crop is planted at all.

Deficiency Payment—Government payment made to farmers who participate in feed grain, wheat, rice, or cotton programs; payment rate is per bushel, pound, or hundredweight, based on the difference between a target price and the market price or the loan rate, whichever results in the smaller payment. *See also* Target Price.

Diversion Payment—A voluntary land retirement option in which farmers are paid for foregone production from their acreage base.

Disaster Payment—Federal aid provided to farmers when either planting is prevented or crop yields are abnormally low as a result of adverse weather and related conditions.

Export Enhancement Program (EEP)—A program whereby the government pays PIK certificates to U.S. exporters who agree to lower the prices of U.S. grain products to buyers in designated countries where U.S. farm products have lost market share as a result of predatory subsidies by other exporting nations.

Family Farm—Legally, a farm that (1) produces agricultural commodities for sale in such quantities so as to be recognized in the community as a farm and not a rural residence; (2) produces enough income (including off-farm employment) to pay family and farm operating expenses, pay debts, and maintain the property; (3) is managed by the operator; (4) has a substantial amount of labor provided by the operator and family; and (5) may use seasonal labor during peak periods and a reasonable amount of full-time labor.

Farm—Defined by the Bureau of the Census in 1978 as any place that has or would have had $1,000 or more in gross sales of farm products.

Farm Credit Administration—The government agency responsible for the supervision, examination, and regulation of the Farm Credit System.

Farm Credit System—A system of borrower-owned banks providing loans to the agricultural sector. Federal Land Banks make long-term farm and rural real estate loans, through local land bank cooperative associations. Federal Intermediate Credit Banks provide funds to production credit associations (PCAs) that make short- and intermediate-term loans to farmers, ranchers and farm-related businesspeople, and commercial fishers. Banks for Cooperatives make loans to all kinds of agricultural and aquatic cooperatives.

Farmers Home Administration (FmHA)—An Agriculture Department agency that provides credit for those in rural America who are unable to get credit from other sources at reasonable rates and terms. The FmHA makes long-term real estate and short- and intermediate-term operating loans to farmers and ranchers; rural housing loans; community development loans for rural facilities; and water and sewer loans to rural communities.

Feed Grain—Also called course grains, they are any of several grains most commonly used for livestock or poultry feed, such as corn, grain sorghum, oats, and barley.

Food Grain—Cereal seeds most commonly used for human food, chiefly wheat and rice.

Food for Peace (Public Law 480)—Enacted in 1954 to expand foreign markets for U.S. agricultural products, combat hunger, and encourage economic development in developing countries. It makes commodities available through low-interest, long-term credit, as donations for famine or other emergency relief, and to countries that agree to undertake agricultural development projects to improve their own food production and distribution systems.

Food Stamp Program—An Agriculture Department program designed to help low-income households buy an adequate, nutritious diet. The program began as a pilot operation in 1961 and was made part of permanent legislation in the Food Stamp Act of 1964.

General Agreement on Tariffs and Trade (GATT)—An agreement negotiated in 1947 among twenty-three countries, including the United States, to increase international trade by reducing tariffs and other trade barriers. The multilateral agreement provides a code of conduct for international commerce. GATT also provides a framework for periodic multilateral negotiations on trade liberalization and expansion. Since 1973 eight sessions have been held, including a current round in Geneva, Switzerland, which began in January 1988. Membership has increased to include ninety contracting nations, thirty-one countries that apply its rules de facto, and one country that has accepted them provisionally. These participants account for 90 percent of world trade.

Import Quota—The maximum quantity or value of a commodity allowed to enter a country during a specified time.

Loan Rate—The price per unit (bushel, bale, or pound) at which the government will provide loans to farmers to enable them to hold their crops for later sale. The loan rate serves as a floor for domestic market prices, because farmers do not have to sell below that level. *See* Nonrecourse Loans.

Mandatory Production Controls—If sanctioned in a national referendum by a majority (or more, in some cases) of farmers of a particular crop, the government determines how much of that crop is needed to fill annual demand and achieve a minimum price, then imposes acreage allotments and marketing quotas on every farmer producing that crop. The government may impose financial penalties on producers who fail to comply with their allotments or quotas.

Marketing Board—A government-controlled trading agency used in some countries (but not in the United States) to sell agricultural products for export. These boards often have a monopoly on their products.

Marketing Loan—The current policy for cotton, rice, and honey. If market prices are below the nonrecourse loan rate, farmers can repay their crop loans at whatever price they can get at market. The farmers keep the balance of the loan principal. *See also* Nonrecourse Loans.

Multilateral Agreement—Trade agreements or programs involving three or more countries, such as the General Agreement on Tariffs and Trade (GATT). *See also* Bilateral Agreement.

Nonrecourse Loans—The government sets a per-bushel loan rate at which farmers can borrow money after harvest, so they can hold their crops for later sale. The crop is the collateral for the loan, and the farmer can either repay the loan and sell the crop, or default on the loan and forfeit the crop to the government. The government has no legal recourse other than acquiring the collateral for getting its money back from the farmer. *See also* Loan Rate.

Parity—Originally a measure of a farmer's purchasing power relative to urban citizens. It is the unit price of a crop that would be needed today to buy the same quantity of a standard list of goods the unit would have bought in the past. The parity bench mark originally was the years 1910-1914—the so-called "golden era" of American agriculture. Now the formula is based on a moving ten-year average. Though no longer used in current farm programs, parity is a goal of mandatory production controls. *See also* Mandatory Production Controls.

Payment-in-Kind (PIK)—Farmers are compensated with government-controlled commodities instead of cash. In 1983 and previous years, the Agriculture Department delivered the actual commodity to farmers on a bushel replacement basis to farmers who took land out of production. In 1986 and succeeding years, the department began issuing PIK certificates with a cash face value, which farmers could redeem for government-controlled commodities at specified prices, which are usually substantially below the government's acquisition price.

Payment Limitation—A limitation set by law on the amount of money any one individual may receive in farm program payments, such as deficiency and disaster payments, each year under the wheat, feed grain, cotton, and rice programs. The limitation is currently $50,000, although it has significant exceptions. For example, there is no limit on the value of loans received or on any gain realized from marketing loans. Certain portions of the deficiency payments, made when the agriculture secretary lowers the loan rate beyond the statutory level, also are not covered by the $50,000 payment limit, although they come under an overall $250,000 payment limit. In 1987 Congress placed restrictions on the ability of farmers to subdivide their land holdings and receive multiple payments under different corporate entities.

Permanent Farm Law—The statutory legislation upon which many agricultural programs are based. For the major commodities, these are the Agricultural Adjustment Act of 1938 and the Agricultural Act of 1949. Although these laws are frequently amended for a given number of years, they would once again become law if current amendments (such as the 1985 farm bill, which expires December 31, 1990) were to lapse without new legislation being enacted.

Program Crops—Storable grain and fiber crops—wheat, corn, soybeans, rice, cotton, barley, oats, and sorghum—for which farmers can receive price-support benefits with certain government conditions. Other farm products supported in various ways by the government are tobacco, peanuts, sugar, honey, wool and mohair, and dairy products.

Set-aside—A program to limit production by restricting the use of land. It restricts the amount of a farmer's total cropland base used for production instead of on the acres used to produce a specific crop. Planting of nonsurplus crops, haying, and grazing could be permitted on set-aside acreage. *See also* Acreage Reduction Program and Base Acreage.

Sodbuster—A program prohibiting farmers from cultivating grasslands or other highly erodible land or risk losing their eligibility for government farm program benefits. A sister "swampbuster" program applies to fragile wetlands.

Supply Management—A policy of government intervention in agriculture to limit surplus production and stabilize prices. The methods involve both voluntary programs, such as when farmers idle a certain percentage of land to qualify for loans and deficiency payments, and mandatory programs. *See also* Mandatory Production Controls.

Target Price—Congress's notion of an ideal price for a particular commodity. When market prices are depressed, the government pays farmers participating in commodity programs the difference between the target and either the average domestic market price or the loan rate, whichever results in the smaller payment. *See also* Deficiency Payments.

Tariffs—A system of duties imposed by a government on imported goods.

Whole Herd Buyout Program—A program requiring the agriculture secretary to accept compensation bids from dairy farmers who are willing to slaughter their herds and retire from production for five years in return for a government payment.

Bibliography

Benedict, Murray R. *Farm Policies of the United States, 1790-1950: A Study of Their Origins and Development.* New York: The Twentieth Century Fund, 1953.

Benson, Ezra Taft. *Freedom to Farm.* Garden City, N.Y.: Doubleday, 1960.

Berger, Samuel R. *Dollar Harvest: The Story of the Farm Bureau.* Lexington, Mass.: Heath Lexington Books, 1971.

Cochrane, Willard W., and Mary E. Ryan. *American Farm Policy, 1948-1973.* Minneapolis: University of Minnesota Press, 1976.

Cochrane, Willard W. *The Development of American Agriculture: A Historical Analysis.* Minneapolis: University of Minnesota Press, 1979.

Commission of the European Communities. *The Agricultural Situation in the Community, 1986 Report.* Brussels, Luxembourg: Office for Official Publications of the European Communities, 1987.

Fite, Gilbert C. *George N. Peek and the Fight for Farm Parity.* Norman, Okla.: University of Oklahoma Press, 1954.

Glaser, Lewrene K. *Provisions of the Food Security Act of 1985.* National Economics Division, Economic Research Service, U.S. Department of Agriculture. Agriculture Information Bulletin No. 498. April 1986.

Hathaway, Dale E. *Agriculture and the GATT: Rewriting the Rules (Policy Analyses in International Economics, 20).* Washington, D.C.: Institute for International Economics, September 1987.

Johnson, D. Gale, ed. *Food and Agricultural Policy for the*

1980s. Washington, D.C.: American Enterprise Institute for Public Policy Research, 1981.

Kennedy, Joseph V., "Generic Commodity Certificates: How They Affect Markets and the Federal Budget." *Choices* (Fall 1987).

Miller, Geoff. *The Political Economy of International Agricultural Policy Reform*. Canberra: Australian Government Publishing Service, 1986.

Organisation for Economic Cooperation and Development. *National Policies and Agricultural Trade*. Paris: Organisation for Economic Cooperation and Development, 1987.

Paarlberg, Robert L. *Fixing Farm Trade: Policy Options for the United States*. Edited by C. Michael Aho. The Council on Foreign Relations Series on International Trade. Cambridge, Mass.: Ballinger Publishing Co., 1988.

Revel, Alain, and Christophe Riboud. *American Green Power*. Translated by Edward W. Tanner. Baltimore, Md.: The Johns Hopkins University Press, 1986.

The World Bank. *World Development Report 1986*. New York: Oxford University Press, 1986.

Index